SPIRITUAL
EVOLUTION

in the

ANIMAL
KINGDOM

KARMA

REINCARNATION

AND THE REPERCUSSIONS OF EATING MEAT

DAVID BARRETO

Editorial Review by Andrew J. Keogh
Cover by David Barreto

First edition: 2021, London, UK.
ISBN: 978-1-9162111-6-2

www.davidbarreto.net
info@davidbarreto.net

SPIRITUAL EVOLUTION

in the

ANIMAL KINGDOM

CONTENTS

INTRODUCTION

Throughout its history, spiritualist literature has hardly questioned the role played by the souls of animals in the spiritual world, apart from some alleged successive reincarnations.

On the limited occasions when animal spirituality has been addressed, the subject matter has customarily been reduced to "evolving beings" or rather mediocre approaches to a certain spiritual "energy" that would animate their physical bodies. Although ancient cultures such as the Hindu and the Egyptian advocated that people could be reincarnated as certain animals,[1] or that various gods have the figure of, for example, an eagle, or even that such animals were sacred, they failed to examine in depth the intrinsic spiritual significance of the species from an egalitarian perspective. Thus, all connotations of animal spirituality have consistently been complementary to human superstition that envisaged to benefit their spiritual journey. "Cats attract luck."[2] "The Elephant God promotes prosperity."[3] "Sacrifice a lamb, for it takes away our sins."[4] "This animal is my guardian animal."[5] As per those examples, it is clear that the remote and the contemporaneous religions and cults have systematically objectified animals, distancing "the beast" from "the sublime".

Frequently, mystical liturgies involving animals are designed to support and favour human spirituality, for most of what has been shown or researched regarding the animals' souls is promptly subjected to human worship and how the animals in question may assist their interests.

Various books attempt to address the subject of the "animal", but the content is usually reduced to interminable lists of which animal signifies what in dreams or mythologies, with other materials merely stating that animals reincarnate, albeit in a less complex manner when compared to humans. In other words, what is found only covers the mere use of their symbolism to further assist humans and their journey towards spiritual ascension and mystical studies.

It is, however, relatively easy to have access to the literature regarding ascended masters, angels and extra-terrestrials who typically dwell far away or in distant dimensions.

In modern days, spiritualist groups, the New Age movement and world religions still seldom debate the significance of animals regarding creation and spiritual enlightenment, reserving such studies to humans only, as though animals were far from being correlated or categorised as kindred spirits.

In both religious and spiritualistic literature and doctrine, karma, universal laws and altruism seem to only have an effect when the interaction occurs between human to human, which wrongfully undermines one's sins or violations against the well-being of animals and their right to live and evolve spiritually.

It has always sounded rather intriguing how humans could exemplify such a vast range of spiritual rights and responsibilities for themselves, but chimpanzees, who share about 99% of DNA with humans,[6] have next to no mention in religious and even mystical scriptures.

Upon failing to get the answers regarding animal spirituality to the same depth that it is available when the subject is humans, I decided to deeply investigate ancient civilisations, folklores and esoteric schools to not only find answers to my questions but to share with the world how immensely important the presence of animals in the spiritual world is, detaching their existence from the advantages they may provide.

Initially, I used my academic expertise to gather information from ancient cultures, anticipating the poor referencing that those books, scriptures and oral mythologies could offer concerning the spirituality of animals. The more I deepened my research into ancient world religions, the more it was clear that animals have never had a prominent status or exceptional treatment, even though animal iconography was and still is vast.

I have reread numerous esoteric books from my collection to identify any allusion to the creation and participation of animals in spiritual phenomena. The result was disappointing. The mentions were reduced to lists of animals and how humans could use their symbols, be spiritually protected by them and how such deities were somewhat connected to those animals. The urge to include animals and their spiritual evolution into esoteric and spiritual disciplines guided me to dedicate time and energy to building this work.

Having participated in several spiritualist sessions and having witnessed countless mediumistic activities, I drew a parallel between the spirits of humans and their alleged paranormal behaviour and the spirits of animals, verifying any similarity and discrepancy. A lifetime of reading books on Western esotericism and the supernatural also validated my assumptions in categorising the spirits of most species found on Earth. It is essential to indicate that the scientific data shown in this work was compared to an esoteric orientation, and that esoteric claims were, similarly, tested with scientific data.

This book also addresses the spiritual repercussions of meat consumption, referring to various spiritualist and metaphysical explanations. Additionally, I was moved to address the impact that the meat industry has on the spiritual evolution of animals, which is often disregarded by those who profit from such misfortune and consume it. The numbed societies that view meat and animal exploitation as the norm need to be addressed, as they study and practice religion and more generally, spirituality, yet choose to ignore the very laws and teachings they claim to obey.

Since astrophysics and cosmology are present in most of my works, I have dedicated the chapters of this book to the scrutiny of those sciences, in an attempt to find common ground and theoretical methods to equate animals to humans.

I have spent over two years examining papers from the most renowned laboratories and universities on the planet, to support the claims on this work that regard scientific research, numbers, experiments, names and historical periods.

Holding educational certifications from the Australian National University and Harvard University, I instinctively applied an objective and neutral approach to my research for this book.

Therefore, this work altruistically presents and investigates the souls of animals under the lens of modern-day and ancient spiritualist outlooks, regardless of what they may represent to humans and their religiosity.

The composition of their spirits is analysed in conjunction with how they evolve spiritually and physiologically. I will elucidate what animals do on the astral plane and how karma interferes in their lives. I will also indicate the psychic powers that various species enjoy in the chapters ahead.

This work focuses on all species of animals, without prioritising one or another species. The metaphysical implications and symbolism in the existence of various animals on this planet are to be interpreted, justifying why absolutely all animals are of unquestionable importance for the Earth's spiritual evolution.

Taking advantage of an association between modern physics and metaphysics, I endeavour to indicate how balance in the terrestrial psychosphere can be achieved through the fraternal treatment of animals, referring to Divine science as a form of undebatable intelligence in Its creations.

Finally, this book addresses the awakening of a new astrological era, where animals will have their earthly lives elevated to lasting worthiness and dignity. Thus, veganism is constructed as the culmination of the Age of Aquarius.*

---

* *The use of common terminology from the fields of physics, chemistry and quantum mechanics is for didactic reasons. Similarities with these aforementioned sciences and theories may be purely or partially coincidental.*

THE SOULS OF ANIMALS

The Source

The creation of a spirit emerges from a creative source, which may be characterised as "God".

Any attempt to explain God is challenging and rather ambitious, as the concept of "God" is inevitably subject to the conditioning of the physical brain. The physical brain, in these lines of thought, exemplifies a reduced valve of consciousness.[1] In other words, the physical brain is the materialised version of consciousness, albeit in a much more reduced constitution, for the experiences in the physical realm.

The physical brain is constituted of approximately 86 billion neurons, yet it is still not able to understand how other planes above the third dimension work, despite having the most complex technological tools at hand.

The physical brain may be considered as a reductionist valve because it reduces perceptions of the environment. When sound is heard, or an image seen, or when smells are recognised, the brain processes and decodes that information exclusively based on the material environment that surrounds it. Thus the brain is a reader of physical phenomena, and therefore it translates vibrations and matter into observable reality.

Each and every explanation of God will depend on the physical brain, which will impeccably try to understand God, albeit in a physical, observational way.

Consciousness is manifested physically as the brain, and although able to acquire significantly more information than its material counterpart, is still in primitive stages of spiritual evolution. This means that, despite enjoying a broader perspective, human consciousness (spirit incarnate as human) still needs to evolve considerably to fully understand God.

Explaining the concept of God to a physical brain is comparable to explaining electricity to a child, whereas explaining electricity to an electrodynamics scholar is comparable to explaining God to an evolved consciousness.

To fully comprehend God, an unimaginable capacity of understanding would be required by the spirits who are incarnated as humans today. However, considering that even spirits with immense evolutionary progress, such as Laozi or the Count of St. Germain, still do not understand God in its total magnitude, nevertheless, they are well on their way to doing so.

Criticism based on Cartesian logic and materialistic sciences alleges that the existence of God cannot be proven[2]. However, God should not be evidenced in the material world through the lenses of a microscope, for God is not matter. The use of materialistic theories to prove that a non-physical being should or should not exist is unproductive and ineffectual.

Intelligence or academic degrees are not prerequisites for the acceptance or denial of possibilities concerning the existence of God, or any extra-physical entity. Correspondingly, microscopes will not see God, satellites will not speak to another dimension and quantum computers will not contact the spiritual world, as these instruments are **material** instruments, made in the **material** world to deal with **material** phenomena.

Presumably, in the future, enlightened scientists will produce interdimensional or 'spiritual' devices, but these technologies are still mere prospects, more specifically associated with the Age of Aquarius.

Creation of the Spirit

The following explanation derives from what a physical brain, as a decoder, may be capable of assimilating.

Although creation occurs in the subtle dimensions, this analysis regards spiritual and astral creation, which are the primal reasons for matter to emerge.

Source, also called God, is consciousness, therefore the creator of reality. Its creation occurs at a quantum level, that is, it invariably starts with the fabrication of minuscule particles and waves before it develops into anything else. These particles and waves will normally give rise to larger and more sophisticated particles and waves.

The quantum vacuum is the quantum state with the lowest possible energy. Generally, it contains no physical particles, and according to quantum mechanics, the vacuum state is not truly empty but instead contains fleeting electromagnetic waves and particles that pop into and out of existence.

In the creation of matter, holographic particles are not physical, but subtle, until they condense as a result of the fundamental forces of nature. Thus, this field alters the vibrational frequency of a given space-time region,[3] and this movement produces tiny holograms of particles and/or waves. Subsequently, the Higgs field gives mass to those tiny holograms, via their own interaction with the Higgs bosons present in the Higgs field. These tiny particles/waves, thus, give rise to holographic bosons, hadrons and fermions, which eventually constitute electrons, photons, baryons, neutrons and protons.[4]

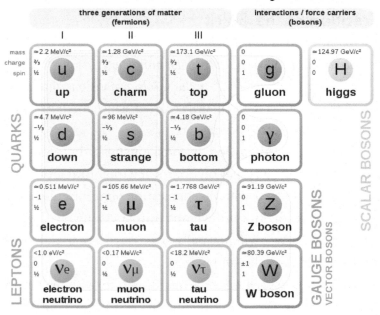

Standard Model of Elementary Particles

The Standard Model of elementary particles, with the gauge bosons (virtual particles) in the fourth column in red. These are smallest particles found in the universe. Credit: Fermi National Accelerator Laboratory, US

At the moment of spiritual creation, that is, of the particles and waves that will not become matter of the third dimension, the Atman is created, or detached from the Source. The Atman can be understood as a holographic particle of God, which will remain holographic forever in relation to the concepts of the third dimension.

The Atman, a "divine spark" not yet connected to any physical form, then begins its journey towards evolution. The Atman, however, is not encapsulated by one sole physical particle, but by trillions of them. The parity between Atman and elementary particles are, thus, not one to one. Even though it is a divine fragment, the Atman is still a simple elementary consciousness at this point. Although the Atman will not gain physical mass, it can be encapsulated by it, thereby experiencing existence in the physical dimension. The physical mass that encapsulates the Atman refers to the elementary particles created from the quantum vacuum and in the Higgs field.

As the physical particles that encapsulate the Atman move from the quantum vacuum to matter, the Divine spark initiates an evolutionary journey to add experience and complexity to itself, thus it may rejoin Source again in a significantly distant future.

Typically, this primitive consciousness would first appear as an elemental of a certain kingdom (mineral, aquatic, aerial, fiery)[5], evolving in the astral dimensions as an "invisible" part of the elements, until it may finally join a rudimentary being in the third dimension.

An elemental is a well-structured form of energy with a minor degree of awareness, who dwells among the astral versions of the earthly elements before eventually merging or migrating to, or as, those elements in the third dimension. Some, however, may never migrate to the physical third dimension.

All beings that inhabit the physical universe initiated their existence correspondingly, originating in one of those kingdoms of matter, thereby being able to start their evolution of consciousness in more ethereal realms before migrating to matter. These consciousnesses will live among stones, water, gas molecules, magma, and subsequently, among plants and insect colonies.

Take into consideration that "consciousness" signifies a prototype of the spirit.

In the physical dimension, evolution results as a consequence of the physical conflicts undergone by these beings over the course of thousands of years. As elementals of stones, water and gases, these beings progressively experience physical pressure, temperature variation and environmental collisions, which leads the immature consciousness to the acquisition of further complexity.[4]

After spending considerable time gathering experiences, the embryonic consciousness that inhabits those rudimentary molecules begins to migrate to more complex kingdoms, where the experiences are compulsorily varied and sophisticated, exemplified in the *monera, protista* and *fungi* kingdoms. In these elementary kingdoms, these beings experience life in the physical dimension for the first time. Thereupon they may reach the *plantae* kingdom, and eventually the *animalia* kingdom.

In the *plantae* kingdom, they will assimilate life by means of fluid exchange, respiration and an immersed union with the physical world, as plants normally depend on water, minerals and, typically, sunlight.

The *animalia* kingdom, however, is the kingdom where the experiences are designed to introduce these embryonic souls to instincts.

The Atman created by God, will sail through different non-physical and physical species before eventually returning to the Source. It will perpetually have an invariable essence, whatever the species or evolutionary level in which it finds itself.

The Atman has the essence of the rudimentary spirit, thus, the essence found in a stone, such as black tourmaline, works its electromagnetism on nefarious energies. That same essence may eventually migrate to a plant that, comparable to the black tourmaline, absorbs harmful energy from the environment.

The mitigation of toxic energies is also the case of plants such as rue. And the essence of rues may likewise animate similar animals like snakes and cats when it migrates to the animal kingdom.

Finally, this snake or cat may come to migrate to the hominid kingdom (not necessarily as Homo sapiens on Earth, but having Adamic characteristics, as opposed to mostly animalistic characteristics). Additionally, they will in turn most certainly become beings who, in many lives, will be committed to protecting others or cleaning environments, such as guards, police officers or recyclers.

The evolutionary level advances and the kingdoms vary, nevertheless, the essence of the being – the Atman – remains unaffected. Thus, the example of the black tourmaline's journey concerns "protection beings". Notwithstanding one's essence, different atmans also comprehend a variety of essences, such as knowledge, faith, love and justice.

The stone, the herb, the animal, the human and the angel repeatedly maintain their essence, therefore they will eternally be unique. Even in the distant future, when these atmans merge back into Source, they will still remain unique.

Aspects or fragments of different species' appearances may be perceived as the common origin of their spiritual essence at creation.

The evolution of these consciousnesses in matter is analogous to the evolution of the species examined in modern-day biology. And just as some prehistoric animals evolved into bipeds until they reached Homo sapiens, the evolution of consciousness on this planet occurs in a corresponding and proportional manner.[4]

The Spiritual Bodies

The spirits that animate humans are composed of six subtle bodies, along with several layers in each of them. However, the variation in the number of subtle bodies in animals may fluctuate, since there is a colossal range of microscopic, single-celled and brainless beings, as well as some the size of cars and the hominids, bearers of amplified intellect.

The bodies which are found in both humans and non-human animals are as follows:

The Physical Body: this is a body that comprises the individual's material components, such as cells, organs and tissues. The glands, whose physiological function includes producing hormones, are found in the physical body. However, they also work as capturing antennas and projectors of electromagnetism in the etheric body. The glands, therefore, personify the bridges that anchor energies of subtle bodies in the physical body.

In unicellular beings, microscopic insects and marine sponges, the physical body is generally the only sophisticated body that they possess, therefore, only a migrating plasma system envelops them, which still cannot be characterised as a complex etheric body.

The plasma system is a field of magnetic currents that surrounds a living being of a certain species. The currents around the living being in question are tenuous early in life, developing stronger in the middle of the being's life and consequently migrating when the being is near its final moments in life. The migration to other familiar beings happens naturally by physical and biological proximity.

The Etheric Body: this body is the semi-physical energy field that lies between the physical body and the astral body. The etheric body has this name by the reason of being considerably subtle, comparable to ether, but it has nothing to do with such an oxygenated compound.

This semi-physical fluid is composed of plasma, loose atoms, photons, gases in small quantities and electromagnetic currents. There are several layers of etheric bodies, some denser than others. The aura which is seen via psychic ability is part of this body.

This body can be understood as a "glue" located in between the physical and the astral bodies, being dissolved after physical death.

The etheric body is the subtle body, of the highest complexity in beings such as insects, starfish, jellyfish and many ordinary fish. In these animals, the etheric bodies host information about the species they are affiliated to and purport to inhabit. The migration occurs purely in the form of waves to other beings at the time of physical death.

Their migration is a morphogenetic field process, which for these animals is the only mechanism of consciousness 'reincarnation' to other animals of similar physical sophistication.

The morphogenetic field is a hypothetical field that would explain the simultaneous emergence of the same adaptive function in non-contiguous biological populations. It would be a kind of instinctive "collective conscious" of the populations, or the idea of mysterious telepathy-type interconnections between organisms and of collective memories within species. This accounts for phantom limbs, how dogs know when their owners are coming home and how people know when someone is staring at them from far away.[6]

Illustration of the dog's seven main chakras, where most point downwards, exchanging energies with the ground.

Substantial parts of the chakras are located in the etheric body. However, the majority of these energy vortices continue to holographically exist in disincarnated spirits, although their aspects and functions are different from the chakras of an incarnated consciousness.

Among the seven main chakras of dogs, cats and other quadrupeds, most of them easily connect to telluric energies, as one of their sides faces downwards. Their four paws on the ground not only reinforce their relation to earthly life but also serve as valves that exchange etheric energies with the ground.

The vast majority of animals have their three lower chakras as their vital chakras, which are designed for survival, i.e. eating, self-preservation, reproduction. Nevertheless, when emotionally connected to humans, a fourth chakra awakens: the heart chakra, which is associated with emotions.

The Astral Body: this is the original matrix of the physical body, endowing it with functions and aspects. This body also carries the biological records of past lives, such as physical traumas, passions and antimatter, which may be purged on a subsequent experience in the physical dimension. The antimatter purged is one of the main components of the so-called "negative energy". The electrical charge of antimatter is generally opposite to that of ordinary matter, such as the electron and positron, the proton and the antiproton. The purge is usually the redeeming of karma debt.

This body is the one that gives physical form to consciousness when it is disembodied.

This body is formed by an identical replica of the physical body, as a hologram that can only be seen in the astral dimension or above. However, the ability of psychics to see astral bodies is usually effortless.

The individual's psyche may shape it, transforming its appearance which, reciprocally, affects the physical body to exhibit that image acquired on astral dimension. However, mutations in the astral body that may produce alterations in the physical body are reliant on DNA. That is, given the astral body has developed wings, these will not materialise in the physical body for obvious reasons. When an individual undertakes plastic surgery or dyes the hair another colour, the astral body usually accompanies the transformation.[4]

When sleeping, the individual typically has this body detached from other bodies, hence the term "astral travel". However, in astral travel, the projector's conscious mind is awakened and, accompanied by the astral body, detaches; and thus they "travel" in unison. In ordinary sleep, the astral body is detached, but consciousness (mind) will not necessarily detach conjointly.

Lucid dreams may be perceived as an astral projection. However, this state suggests that the conscious mind has little lucidity, managing to only retain a certain limited amount of information. Occasionally, the information in the unconscious mind takes shape during the dream, turning the lucid dream's scarce lucidity into a reverie-like dream.

The dream, in turn, is generally a series of old and new memories transported from the subconscious mind to the conscious mind. Usually, animals of significant physical size may have lucid dreams, and this phenomenon occurs based on the density of white matter in their brains' cortex.

The neocortex contains cells that produce sensations such as sights and sounds when no stimuli are coming from outside. To replicate such astral and subconscious sensations, the animal must have a relevant breadth of neocortex to assimilate the signs and sounds coming from another dimension and from remote parts of their brains. Since the presence of the neocortex is indispensable for dreams to occur, reptiles, amphibians and fish do not dream. Keep in mind that, along with the neocortex, animals need an astral body for the dream to occur.[4] Allowing that the brain is the physical version of consciousness, albeit, in a reduced version, it is understood that animals with an insufficiently developed astral body cannot dream, since the prototypes of their astral bodies do not detach from the others and, thus, their instincts still completely dominate the functions of their brains, which do not yet assimilate individuality.

The astral body is made up of multidimensional holographic particles, which includes baryons, leptons and neutrinos. Were these condensed physical molecules, they would be relative to molecules that constitute silicon dioxide, since the two elements have acutely similar frequency amplitudes, albeit in different dimensions.

It is in this body that magic spells against the individual take place. Likewise, this is the subtle body of sensitive mediums that spirits and entities attach to for mystical channelling.

The astral body is generally the most sophisticated subtle body that reptiles may own. Any auxiliary subtle body found in this species, besides the astral, would be simply a set of collective currents and/or embryonic systems of an astral body. Amphibians and types of fish also have this as their most refined subtle body, which is characterised by a shallow individualisation.

The Lower Mental Body: this body is a spherical wave that interpenetrates the other six bodies. In most species of animals, including humans, it is located between the navel and two feet above the head. This is also an elastic body, which is invariably much longer than the physical body.

Although this body is mostly seen as an oval sphere in humans, its form can easily be moulded into virtually any form, including that of the astral body.

It is responsible for thoughts and reasoning, the subconscious and the sense of "right and wrong", being the non-material counterpart of the brain concerning emotions. This is the body where thought-forms are produced, which, once nourished by the astral body, are exteriorised.

This body is composed of highly subtle plasma.

For most mammals, as well as most birds, this is the most developed subtle body in their current evolutionary levels. Domesticated animals, such as dogs, cats, horses and monkeys, frequently strengthen these bodies thoroughly during their physical lives.

The Upper Mental Body: this body is responsible for the sublime thoughts and ideas detached from materialism. It is also the part of the individual that expresses the essence of consciousness by virtue of their personality.

The upper mental body is often constructed in a manner that resembles helices or long petals. It is divided into ten parts in humans and three parts in the vast majority of other mammals. These "petals" are connected to other subtle bodies employing energy cords. Although these petals give form to this body, the upper mental body does not have a defined shape, but it appears this way so that humans endowed with mediumship can understand it when in a mediumistic trance or in astral projection.

Helix number 1 is connected to the buddhic body in humans, with a direct tie to consciousness and past lives beyond 700 years. In animals, this helix still has an embryonic quality. Helix number 2 is linked to intuition, carrying information from experiences that occurred between 300 and 700 years ago. Only a small number of animals, usually quadrupeds, have this helix relatively developed, albeit almost constantly inactive. Helix number 3 is connected to the morals of the conscience, and it contains the memories of incarnations from the past 300 years. This helix attaches to the lower mental body. Mammals, such as dogs, dolphins, pigs and chimpanzees, have this "petal" comparatively similar to that of human souls. Helices 4 and 7 are attached to the astral body, absorbing and sending information. The process and functionality of these petals in the upper mental body of mammals and birds are identical to their functions in humans. Helices 5 and 6 are connected to the astral body (and prototypes of astral bodies) of all vertebrate animals, in a system identical to the process in humans. Helices 8 and 9 are connected to the Atman body. In animals, these helices are still small sparks in a rudimentary state. Helix number 10 is the centre of this fan or flower bud, or the core of this body, where the energies of spiritual healing make their first stop before being distributed to other bodies, including the physical body. Do not confuse spiritual healing with energising or energetic cleansing – which takes place directly in the astral and etheric bodies.

The colours of this body vary from helix to helix in the souls of humans, each colour being a sign of the health and state of each body whose specific helix is linked to. In animals, adversely, this "flower" is ordinarily sparkling white with hues of pink and blue.

The upper mental body, which has no material counterpart, is entirely independent of physical existence or the third dimension. It is composed of a high-frequency field that operates in several dimensions simultaneously. Animals have yet to develop this body and experience most of its qualities, however, it already exists to a superficial degree in most mammals.

The Buddhic Body: this body is also known as "buddhi", where memories from the beginning of the individual's creation are stored. This sun-shaped body is an authentic software for recording consciousness. Numerous species of animals have it; however, it is comparable to a wave of information rather than a well-structured body. Thus, the buddhic body of animals may be recognised as a holographic cell that, eventually, will embellish a sophisticated anatomy.

All vertebrate animals have this corpuscle in the shape of a small spark, which agglutinates to their other bodies.

The buddhi also functions as a compass that measures when and how a discarnate spirit must reincarnate in order to repair the imbalances in its evolutionary and expanding journey. In animals where such a body is an elementary model, the rhythm in which their astral or etheric bodies should behave is the Buddhi's attribution. Moreover, it is through the buddhic body that the spiritual guides and mentors communicate.

The constitution of the buddhi is forged by multidimensional fields networks.

The Atman Body: this shapeless body is known in Gnosticism as the "divine spark". It is also the first element that detached from "Source" to start its individual expansion. The Atman initiates its existence in the divine dimension, subsequently delving into the spiritual dimension.

All sorts of animals, both multicellular and unicellular, are a divine spark. What varies is its functions concerning each species. In primitive species, typically communities of insects, each Atman is encapsulated by a collective aggregation of physical and semi-physical elements, resulting in a

collective journey until each insect migrate to another kingdom in evolution.

In the spark resides the perfect essence of the monad,
which in Cosmogony refers to the Supreme Being or the divinity within.

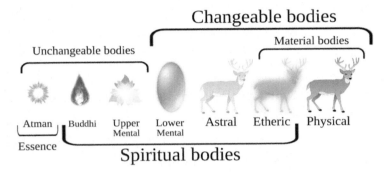

The evolution of the animals' spirits in the third dimension
occurs proportionally to the "evolution of the species" whereby
a given species undergoes adaptive mutations, sophisticating
their bodies and senses. It must be stressed that the same
process has happened and will continue to happen to humans.
Nevertheless, physical changes over the millennia do not
happen unexpectedly, but by the influence of consciousness
that animates the physical body.

Sequentially, the evolution of the spirit inclines to the
knowledge acquired, along with noble morals, such as compassion, benevolence and empathy. In other words, love.

As an example, the spirits that animate frogs, whose Atman
origins are identical to those of humanoid spirits, must also
develop their physical bodies to obtain enough spiritual expansion, thereby being able to make compassionate decisions

and progress to transcendence. It must be taken into consideration that although humans can develop such qualities, a large proportion of the world's population remains dormant to them; therefore, being human does not automatically classify them as superior to spirits of non-human animals.

The souls of animals, therefore, are notably similar to the souls that animate humans. Many of the spirits that animate humans also initiated their individualised journeys elsewhere in the cosmos, as in other planets; however, the divine spark of each one was generated in a similar course to that of all existing animals.

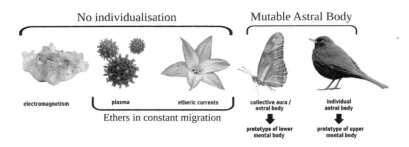

No individualisation   Mutable Astral Body

electromagnetism   plasma   etheric currents   collective aura / astral body   individual astral body

Ethers in constant migration

prototype of lower mental body   prototype of upper mental body

KARMA AND REINCARNATION

Animal Karma

Karma and reincarnation of spirits that animate humans, primarily refers to the repairing of personality imbalances and actions, necessary for that spirit to learn. The karmic process results in potentially painful experiences, but it also comprises the path to love, charity, knowledge and the divine laws.

Karma is a word from Sanskrit that means "action". This is an action that has to be performed or experienced, so one heals their spiritual malaise, that is, the imbalance between the principles of Action and Reaction, caused by moral failure or misconduct, either in past lives or in their current ones.

Karma drives an individual to encounter a similar emotional experience for the action that has been caused. One does not necessarily experience the very same reaction to the action initially taken, but an experience that emotionally corresponds to the pain one might have caused.

Karma can also be reparative, signifying that the individual acts directly in the reaction to "solve" that adverse action caused. As an illustration, a false priest, a false medium or an individual with the ability to persuade by the agency of faith may inexcusably direct a devout community to infelicitous paths, for their own individual benefit and the gaining of power. The karma of these false spiritual leaders could be, imaginably, having the obligation of dedicating themselves in the next life to directing a community to compassionate paths, either as a self-help speaker, a sincere priest, a psychologist or as an educator, thus causing a repairing effect contrary to what has been caused originally. Most of these educators and priests who come to devote their lives to teaching humanitarian conduct certainly enjoy what they do, despite its difficulties. Thus karma is not necessarily a burden, but a condition.[1]

The karma a person goes through is nothing more than "rebalancing their vibrational debt in the universe".

As this is hardly achieved due to pungent egos, there is moderate friction as a course of reacting to the impact caused, generating some of what is recognised as "suffering".

Typically, karma is the reaction of an "evil" caused to someone or something, such as the malicious pollution of a river or the cutting of forests for selfish gain. The difference between doing "good" and doing "evil" is that, when doing good, an expansive movement of the spirit is generated, while "bad" actions retain it. Furthermore, the difference between "good" and "bad" is when an individual with the ability to distinguish the two consciously chooses one side. The "good" aims at the benefit of everyone, detached from selfish reasons. The bad, in turn, is characterised by selfishness, where the benefit is only personal, whatever the repercussions for others.

By doing what is appropriately called "evil", there is stagnation and loss of momentum (speed) in the spirits' evolution, which culminates in involuntary actions caused by one's own conscience, that forces the necessary expansion through pain, either emotional or physical.

The more altruistic a person is, the more expanded their consciousness. It expands as a result of benevolent conduct and the knowledge one acquires. This increase in width occurs due to the consciousness' need for greater amplitude for comporting more information.[1]

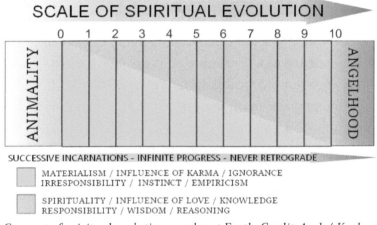

SCALE OF SPIRITUAL EVOLUTION

0 1 2 3 4 5 6 7 8 9 10

ANIMALITY

ANGELHOOD

SUCCESSIVE INCARNATIONS - INFINITE PROGRESS - NEVER RETROGRADE

MATERIALISM / INFLUENCE OF KARMA / IGNORANCE
IRRESPONSIBILITY / INSTINCT / EMPIRICISM

SPIRITUALITY / INFLUENCE OF LOVE / KNOWLEDGE
RESPONSIBILITY / WISDOM / REASONING

Concept of spiritual evolution on planet Earth. Credit: André Koehne

The expansion may also be achieved via quantum leaps, when karma is attenuated by appreciable effort or worthwhile expansion of consciousness in one single life experience. As an example, a heroic act may lead to a quantum leap. The occurrence of quantum leaps is, however, extremely rare.

In quantum theory, the idea of quantum jumps was first introduced by Danish physicist Niels Bohr. The event unfolds when a particle is located in a certain orbit and then it gains a considerable amount of energy, thus the particle jumps to an orbit above.

An interesting phenomenon regarding that leap was that when the electron passes from one orbit to another, it simply disappears from the former and reappears in the next, which elucidates a leap.[2]

The relationship between human and animal karma is, however, typically generated by different factors. The karma that most humans collect in their experiences are karmas that redirect and lead these spirits to repair the deviations in the conduct of past or current incarnations. In the case of animals, karma is natural actions that lead them to expand consciousnesses (spirits) as a consequence of carnal experiences and, often, through physical pain that also affects humans, but in different ways. In these lines, animal karma is just a new experience, instead of a corrective reaction.

An uncomplicated form of understanding animal karma can be applied to all animals endowed with an astral body. These animals do generate karma, nevertheless, the karma generated corresponds to the universal laws of Cause and Effect only.

The difference between the law of 'karma' and the law of 'cause and effect' is that, in karma, a complex event is planned to establish the repair of a fault, whereas in 'cause and effect', the individual is part of a natural movement of forces, where what they project cause an impact in the universe, which reacts back proportionally.

Through physical ordeals, the animal learns about all existing feelings, including pain, fear and anguish. The karmic reasons referring to the pain that animals experience in their journey do not justify, from a spiritual perspective, humans inflicting any harm on them. All animals are incarnated spirits developing the intelligent principle, thus they follow the same path that humans have been following for thousands of years.

Equally to humans, who have entered the hominid scale, animals will eventually do so. They will not necessarily become humans; nevertheless, animals of all sorts will evolve to incarnate in an advanced Hominidae family, either on this planet or another.

Although highly intelligent primates, numerous humans use their intellectual capacities to satisfy their egos in barbaric attitudes. Thus, the karmic responsibility they assume when interfering violently and abusively in the lives of animals is inescapably enormous. On causing suffering via cruelty and exploitation, humans bear the burden of moral deviations and the lack of love which, if not acquired through kindness, must be acquired through the forced purge of these nefarious activities. This purge is also known as "suffering". In other words, the human will unquestionably experience karma for the manner they mistreat animals.

The pain animals encounter, which in some way may contribute to the expansion of their consciousness, does not depend on human actions. That is, humans will not help animals evolve by causing them physical pain, but they will, contrarily, increase their own karma and prevent animals from experiencing every year that their physiology determines (a pig, for instance, can live to be 20 years old, but is taken to be slaughtered before the age of six months in the meat industry).

All forms of malicious suffering inflicted upon an animal, as well as towards another human being, result in serious responsibilities, including the impediment of the universe's conscious expansion.

Despite not all the incarnated spirits having initiated their spiritual journeys or all their spiritual growth on Earth, this study focuses on the explanation concerning this planet.

The universe expands both spiritually and physically, in what cosmologists call metric expansion. Spirits, likewise the species they animate, evolve on Earth coincidentally.

Animals often experience pains and agonies, and these feelings may lead to a certain expansion of consciousness. Animal karma, therefore, is attributed to the experiences they collect to permanently understand the variation of density between dimensions.

It is also valid to reiterate that extreme pains were likewise experienced by humans when their spirits were allocated in different kingdoms, either on this planet or on another. Physical pain is part of the learning process in the third dimension, and as the spirit is eternal, the painful period one spends in the third dimension is usually considered short and fruitful.

Nevertheless, the suffering which humans may cause to animals neither helps nor accelerates their spiritual evolution. Pain is not invariably mandatory in the animals' current evolutionary course. In addition, animals do need to experience their instincts and nature. Moreover, many of them must experience affection. If animals are denied such resources, their experiences will be incomplete, and more metaphysical debt will be associated with the cruel human being.

Such pains are exceedingly incompatible with the category of experiences they need for their evolutionary progress during a single lifetime. No existent universal or divine laws dictate such suffering as animals endure at the hands of humans. All wickedness against animals is unequivocally the result of sheer selfishness.

Reincarnation Process

Human consciousness has reached a certain evolutionary stage in which their essence will always animate a body physically equipped to perform the necessary functions that that consciousness needs to comprehensively experience life, thus being able to assimilate and express all the functions already acquired by the spirit.

By comparing the body and consciousness of a dog with the body and consciousness of a human being, it is understood that the bodies of each are the physical manifestations of their own consciousness. In other words, each spirit will only be compatible with the physical body whose consciousness can exercise all the functions they have already acquired.

A dog's consciousness cannot inhabit a human body before it undergoes a systematic preparation, since the human's consciousness is what generates such a body type relative to humans. Impartially, the consciousness that inhabits a human body cannot inhabit a dog's body, as the animal's body does not have the necessary properties to hold or express the consciousness of the humanoid spirit. The reason is that the structural composition of the human body, namely glands, organs, brain functions and the existence of a thick layer of the neocortex is physiologically more complex than that of the dog.

Note: Although interincarnation between the aforementioned species is less common than reincarnation between spirits in the same species, such a process is not impossible, given the spiritual arrangements and preparatory measures. Cases of domestic animals passing into the hominid kingdom are usually observed by mediums and explained through channelled messages. Especially after the animal accumulates long experience among groups of spiritual rescue, they promote the migration of the animal to the hominid kingdom. It is also common that, in spiritual communities in the astral realms, specific sections are responsible for preparing domesticated animals for future life as humans. However, it is not possible for the human to reincarnate as an animal on this planet.

Human ancestors, e.g. *Australopithecines*, *Homo erectus* and *Homo sapiens*, have all inhabited physical bodies that matched their respective levels of consciousness. Just as those species evolved into the modern *Homo sapiens sapiens*, so simultaneously did their consciousnesses.[3]

Consciousness normally re-inhabits the physical bodies of the same species it had in its previous incarnation, which is compatible with their current spiritual evolutionary levels. This is a norm, nevertheless spirits also migrate to more complex earthly species closely related to what they might have been in their previous existence, albeit never retrogressing.

Evolution via reincarnation is a gradual and natural process, similar to the "evolution of species" in biology, albeit non-perpetual.

Spirits of extinct species commonly reincarnate in their related, more sophisticated family species. This was the case with mammoths to elephants, as well as extinct tiger species to other species close to felines with more intellect. The reason for the extinction of natural origin is essential for the development of these spirits, which mature in more advanced sensory capacities, requiring a more adequate physical body to support such an increase in consciousness. The same principle applies to animals that are victims of man-made extinction. However, the karmic penalties undoubtedly fall on whoever bears responsibility for such abnormal causality.

During the latest period of the Palaeolithic Age (2.5m–10,000 BCE), humans would consider wolves to be their rivals, as the animals would not only hunt the same prey as humans, but they would also attempt to hunt humans themselves.

Naturally, wolves would hunt in packs. Nonetheless, some of them eventually started to get closer to the humans, realising that when they showed a more docile attitude, they could potentially be given leftovers.

As a consequence of the approximation between the two species, proto dogs first appeared around 33 thousand years ago. Those proto dogs were smaller than wolves and exhibited a more gentle temperament, with traits of dependency. Their final domestication occurred circa 14,000 BCE.

During Victorian England, neoteny, which results from the selection of breeds for tameness traits, became common. New breeds of dogs were bred for different purposes, such as hunting, racing, herding, and companionship.

The phenomenon of artificially creating new breeds, as well as the natural occurrence of physiological evolution, coextensively accompanied the spiritual evolution of those canine spirits, from wolves to dogs and from the common dog to its subspecies.

The creation of new breeds was not an achievement of men, but an achievement of the numerous spirits who came to be incarnated in such appropriate bodies. It is worth emphasising that the artificial creation of new breeds was an effect and not a cause. Humans, in such a context, served to facilitate the arrival of a new era for the canine species. The domestication, tameness, and personality traits that dogs achieved through millennia via either method are solely a reflection of the spiritual journey that those spirits needed to experience. The physically sophisticated brains and the detriment of some of their instincts, when compared to wild wolves, served to properly encapsulate a less animalistic facet of those spirits, allowing them to fully express their spiritual virtuousness alongside humans and finally progress to higher realms of spiritual evolution.

Reincarnation materialises in different directions, depending on the species. In a species that may only possess magnetic currents involving their bodies as opposed to souls, as is the case of unicellular beings and microscopic insects, reincarnation may initiate even before their actual physical deaths. Although they do not have a complex energetic structure, the plasma surrounding these beings' atoms vibrates at collective frequencies. This means that what has been lived and experienced by those microscopic beings is not lost as an experience, nor is it stored as a memory.

The plasma that surrounds them is part of the environment that prepares them to eventually obtain spiritual individuality. Preceding death, the plasma that surrounds them migrates to other groups of living beings who live in collectivity. This migration develops through electromagnetic waves.

Even in the animals who are holders of a sophisticated group of etheric bodies or an astral body, which is the case with insects, reptiles and amphibians, reincarnation is also immediately after death. Their reincarnation process is randomised, as their subtle bodies migrate to fertilised eggs in the first stages of development.

The insect's subtle body penetrates the egg instantly at the time of fertilisation. In comparison, a snake only migrates completely to the new body in the egg when most of the new animal's instinctual functions are mature. However, at the time of fertilisation of the egg, the snake's astral body decreases in size so that it can bind to the replicating cells of the future embryo. Additionally, moments after physical death, the snake's essence will induce the pre-fertilised egg with its traits. The time variation that insects, reptiles and amphibians take to connect to an egg for their reincarnation ranges from ¼ of a second to 170 hours.

The more sophisticated the animal's subtle body is, the later they "merge" with another physical body.

These animals' astral and etheric bodies adapt according to the size, shape and gestational stage of the new physical body, which will be animated in a new life. The process of adapting to the new body is also immediate and the cords that connect a recently disembodied spirit to a physical body, typically in eggs, are initiated by wires that connect to each other, like a type of transference systems of holographic data.

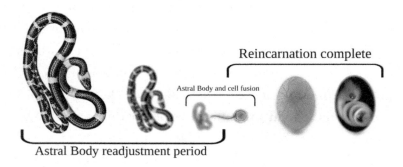

Reincarnation process of a snake. The conscientious transfer of snakes to the eggs is usually immediate after physical death, where their astral body shrinks to the size of cells.

Following the disembodiment of mammals, their spirits remain in the astral dimension indefinitely. However, in most cases the process of reincarnation promptly begins hours after death for some and even years for others, as for the domesticated mammals.

The reincarnation process, which varies from species to species of mammals, occurs in a similar fashion to the process that humanoid spirits undergo. The subtle bodies of the reincarnating spirit gradually connect to the developing zygote. The connection between the reincarnating spirit and the embryo is made by fine energetic threads, which influence the dividing cells and, consequently, give the animal its unique features. In this phase, the activation of inherent spiritual qualities occurs, as well as the activation and inactivation of genes. Until the first moments of gestation, many viviparous animals can still be seen outside the womb of the mother, maintaining the shape of their past lives. Over the course of hours, depending on the species, the animal is immersed in a torpor, where its conscience will remain asleep until birth. The threads that connected the spirit to the embryo, which were previously thin, are now thicker and cause an attraction between the two, which culminates in the joining of the spirit to the foetus in its entirety.

In the case of humans, the process is identical. However, the preparation of the parents' reproductive cells is done even before the spiritual connection.

As humans reincarnate, among other reasons, to collect their karmas and revise family commitments, the spirits of the parents and the reincarnate initially agree for the pregnancy to occur.

A specific sperm is activated, as is the egg that it will find. Until the first weeks of gestation, the individual still sees themselves as their form in the previous life; however, over the weeks they feel numb, in a state of deep sleep. During this phase, their spiritual body is as small as the foetus. The cords that connect both the spirit and the foetus thicken, which culminates in the attraction of the little spirit to intrauterine life.

Intelligent, emotional and domesticated animals do not choose to be reincarnated, nor when they will do so. Supported by friendly spirits, their astral meridians are interwoven with the atoms that are going to develop into the glands of an embryo, which gradually start to animate those bodies on the physical dimension. As their astral bodies temporarily lose the memories from their previous experience in matter, the new body commences receiving the subtle and unique qualities of the spirit.

The reincarnation context of mammals who have thick layers of grey brain matter, or those with any congenital ability to intellect, or moderately inclined to affection, is considerably refined. Such animals, including chimpanzees, dogs and elephants, experience a preparatory process before reincarnating. Their astral bodies carry abundant emotional and intellectual experiences acquired in their previous lives, thus the time they spend in the astral dimension is generally longer than for the majority of other animals.

Usually, dogs and cats remain at their owners' homes as if nothing has changed for a short period after their deaths and preceding a new incarnation (on average, for approximately five weeks). The period in which the spirits of animals remain at their owners' home is orchestrated by friendly spirits.

Thus, when domesticated animals die, they still need to interact with humans in the astral dimensions, due to being accustomed to them when they were alive. For this reason, almost all domesticated animals remain in the homes of their humans for some time after death, and others are taken to spiritual colonies where, in addition to animals of the same species and similar breeds, they can also find the spirits of humans.

After the physical death, it is also common for spiritual mentors to create holographic places and objects familiar to the pet, to make them feel comfortable in the new reality. These holograms are exclusively experienced by the animals' minds.

Occasionally, friendly spirits committed to animals take them to another dimension, to experience the place where other animals of the same species are, and where they will stay until the next reincarnation. From time to time these spirits transport them back to the owner's home. Thus, the animals can get used to the new reality without the trauma of separation.

Differently, when wild dogs and wild cats die, they are usually reincarnated swiftly after their death, as the non-interaction with humans prompts them to a new experience without depending on interaction with alien species.

In hospitals in the astral dimensions, the disoriented spirits of humans may be aided by the spirits of past pets, who are brought by candid nurses to help the deceased humans accept their condition and reduce their sadness about having died.

It is appropriate to add that spirits dedicated to the cause of animals in the astral dimensions commonly influence incarnated humans, so that they help animals in the physical dimension, as rescuers and, less frequently, as activists.

In nature, practically every species progresses close to the ones of the same species. However, when interaction with humans exists, domesticated animals develop affection for another species different from their own. Therefore, these animals greatly amplify their heart chakras, which is relatively compact in most wild animals.

It is doubtlessly possible that the human may find the deceased animal in the astral realm, either via astral travel or after their own deaths. It is also natural for the human to acquire a new pet, which could be the reincarnation of an animal they have had in the past. Another common situation concerns both reincarnating for new experiences together, and although this reunion depends on how important this would be for their evolution, this is a common circumstance.

Interestingly, the intrinsic intelligence of animals such as dolphins, crows and octopuses, does not automatically qualify them for a particularly sophisticated reincarnation process, such as the processes experienced by gorillas and cats. Despite being smart and holders of what transpires to be reasoning, they still need to further develop affection. It is, therefore, the affection that determines which experience the animal must undergo in the next incarnated experience. The less inclined to affection the animal is, the more random the reincarnation may be. However, the more inclined to affection, the more specific the new experience in the flesh must be, to accommodate the emotional needs of that spirit.

Additionally, even though the vast majority of animals reincarnate rapidly after death, not everyone will do so. Some animals, on rare occasions, may take hundreds of years.

Some animals work together with groups of rescue spirits, whereas other spirits of animals join those beings who have never lived incarnated lives. They dwell in dimensions exceptionally close to the third dimension and are customarily called "elementals" of nature.

The elementals are responsible for maintaining the balance between the elements of the planet, stabilising the frequencies between the physical and semi-physical world, and support the movement of life. This is partially executed by those animals that are endowed with plasma instead of a sophisticated soul, which are mostly insects, but also some types of fish, amphibians and reptiles.

The decision to not reincarnate is not the animals', it is, however, due to a natural energetic repair that their souls or subtle bodies must experience momentarily. Occasionally that serves the animal when they are approaching the migration to another realm.

To conclude, wild animals will most likely incarnate into animals raised by humans, such as cattle – hence, no longer being killed by other wild animals but instead, unfortunately by humans. Upon progressing to another species, the cattle will presumably incarnate into other animals kept in captivity, including domesticated animals. Subsequently, they will incarnate into pets such as dogs, cats, and horses. Finally, at least on planet Earth, they will incarnate as humans.

The better humans treat animals, the faster the latter evolves spiritually and progresses to another kingdom, such as that of humans, since animals must understand and deeply interact with the species before they can incarnate as part of them. If animals are mistreated or abused, they will most certainly need more incarnations, until they fully develop emotional bonds.

If humans do support animals in evolving, the human acquires merits. Nevertheless, if humans delay the evolution of animals by being cruel towards them, abusing them or killing them, they will inevitably acquire karmic debt.

Daily, 0.3% of human births are births of former animals (spirits who were animals in their previous life). Considering that, in the first decades of the 21st century, approximately

380 thousand humans were born every day, it is assumed that around one thousand animals delve into the humanoid kingdom every day. Human-first-timers frequently live shorter lives or may occasionally display physiological anomalies.

ANIMALS AND METAPHYSICS

Animal metaphysical energy refers to a complex system of waves and quasi-particles that is generated and usually modified by their subtle bodies and electromagnetic fields.

Extrasensory capabilities

Most vertebrate animals are born with a pineal gland. This physical gland receives the signals of light and darkness from the eyes, thus producing melatonin, which is a hormone related to the sleep pattern. The astral version of this gland, on the other hand, is sensitive to the photons in the electromagnetic field generated and perceived by the physical gland itself. As a result, it produces a wave motion that interferes with the animal's entire electromagnetic field.

The wave interference is established according to the mineral arrangement that composes the apatite in their pineal glands, in that case, calcium phosphate, magnesium phosphate, ammonium phosphate and, especially, calcite. The waves emanating from the apatite, thus, vibrate in alignment with the geometric distribution of its atoms. What makes the calcite exceptional is the crystal's ability to generate an electric current. This ability is known as the "piezoelectric effect".

Piezoelectricity is the electrical charge that accumulates in certain solid materials, such as crystals, types of ceramics and also in biological matter, such as in bones, DNA and various proteins, as a result in response to an applied mechanical stress.[1]

With regard to calcite, due to the pressure that calcium carbonate blades cause on one another, a low-intensity electrical voltage occurs continuously. When the plates push against each other, they direct the loaded parts to their opposite sides. Thus, the positive charge tries to pull electrons from the inner part of the mineral sheets, while the negative part tries to repel the electrons. In such an alternating transit, electricity is generated. The movement, therefore, replicates a geometrically perfect electromagnetic field, propagating the mineral's atomic arrangements.

The piezoelectric effect turns the pineal gland into an illustrative living being, which pulsates the calcite's subatomic holograms unceasingly. The patterns pertinent to the other minerals present in the crystal also contribute to the symmetrical designs that the gland radiates as an electromagnetic field. The crystals' vibration carries the subatomic information as their "genes", which are all pure, perfectly balanced and symmetrically aligned.

Although humans also have a pineal gland, an apprehensive intellect or an exalted ego may repress this gland from exercising its fundamental role as an extra-physical antenna. In most humans, metaphysical signals are unnoticed or ignored. Also, when not utterly discredited, intuition is often implied as a mere guess based on memories or physical instincts.

Cats may not possess greater psychic ability than a human, however, they instinctively use it fully, whereas the human uses a mental filter before astral information is allowed to blossom.

The waves of ether, which is a subtle element – denser than light but thinner than hydrogen – are distributed via vibrational networks that interpenetrate other dimensions, including the physical third dimension, which is evidently inhabited by physical beings. The etheric dimension is the dimension of energies, aura, holographic particles and vital fluid.

The subtlety of etheric waves can be observed by ordinary humans. That is, the individual does not necessarily need to be a psychic medium. Meditation is generally a resource that can be used so that the "ordinary" individual may be capable of capturing and decoding the energies of other dimensions.

It is, however, imperative to acknowledge that the etheric dimension is the closest subtle dimension for the inhabitants of the Earth's third dimension.

Metaphysical Interactions: animal – environment

The ether absorbed and exhaled by insects, as well as by other large animals, will unquestionably interact with humans' electromagnetic fields.

Energy travels to the body's organs, tissues and physical fluids via the energy force centres and the meridians of the humans' semi-physical bodies. This energy, commonly called by different cultures vital energy, *chi/qi* or *prana*, is generated by five different sources:

The macrocosmic energy: this energy is the elastic energy stored by the individuals' auric field and manifested by the environment in which they live. The interaction with the environment, that is, cleaning the house, self-hygiene, sleeping hours and material comfort in the home, all affect this type of energy.[2]

When the macrocosmic energy of the environment is attracted to the individual's auric field, it immediately becomes part of it.

Homes and, without exception, all physical vicinities comprehend an electromagnetic network. While the house may be measured as matter and particle, it can also be measured as energy and wave. Thus, these wave fields carry information regarding the nature of the house's matter and particles. The waves of a disorganised or dishevelled house carry information of chaos and imbalance.

These chaotic energies influence the elastic energy of the individual's auric field, which, as a means to compensate the corrosive circumstance, expands itself, nevertheless becoming scattered.

As all semi-physical elements have limits on how far they can withstand distortion, they are not capable of coping without altering their intrinsic structure. Nevertheless, the essence of elasticity is reversibility, the individual may recover the field's lost particles by simply decluttering, replacing a mattress or by including plants and pleasant pictures in the house.[2]

Such energy is the same for both animals living in the wild and for domestic animals.

The ancestral energy: this is the radiant energy carried by light and thermal energy. Individuals inherit it from ancestors by the route of DNA, in electrical signals between the chromosomes' base pairs.

In complicated molecules like chromosomes, low-lying excited states, such as vibrational motions, take place at each chemical bond, like those between hydrogen and other atoms in the base pairs of DNA, with frequencies ranging from infrared to microwaves. In turn, these motions cause the charge on molecules to move, producing local electrical currents.[3, 4, 5, 6]

Electrical pulses assist chromosome base pairs in message transmission. These pulses become closely linked to the individual during fertilisation and throughout the gestational period. The frequency of electrical pulses between the double helices of the ancestors' chromosomes are thus passed from generation to generation, hence their offspring inherits radiant energy.[2]

The respiratory energy: this is the respiratory kinetic energy of the movement and the flow that the lungs project into the body. This energy is both voluntary and involuntary, this system being the only one in the human body to have both characteristics. The vortex generated by such energy is air-related, not only with regard to matter, but also to what hermetically relates to the mind and thought-forms.

The whirlwind of waves is generated by an assortment of hadrons, whence virtually all of the mass of ordinary matter originates.

The food energy: this is the chemical energy released when the calories of food are consumed by the digestive system.

Alternatively, food energy may be explained as the chemical energy that animals gain via the process of cellular respiration.

Cellular respiration may involve the chemical reaction of food molecules with molecular oxygen in aerobic respiration or via the process of reorganising food molecules without additional oxygen, in anaerobic respiration. Conjointly with calories, food energy offers the molecular and atomic constitution of food, which also manifests the quality of energy that is transmitted as information. When eating, the physical body absorbs the particle, as the etheric body absorbs the wave of it and, consequently, the information encountered.

The interpersonal energy: this is the potential energy stored by the individual's compound field, generated by the auric fields of individuals physically and emotionally close to them.

This type of energy is commonly called "field electrostatics", where the set of charges between the mental and emotional fields of the individual and their companions generate a potential system of repulsion or attraction.[2]

In these lines, the interaction with insects and other animals occurs, most of the time, via the energies mentioned.

Insects and harmful bacteria in the house are attracted by energy imbalances arising from the place's disharmony. Despite the physical and natural reasons why an insect may appear, e.g. food crumbs, holes in the walls and particular climate, it is indisputable that such disorder only unfolds on the physical plane as it is already a reality in the individual's etheric, mental and emotional planes.

Bacteria

Bacteria are single-cell organisms that are neither plants nor animals, and live both inside and outside organisms. They are thought to be the first beings to have appeared on Earth, around four billion years ago. Some bacteria produce oxygen, which played a vital role in creating the oxygen in Earth's atmosphere.

Types of bacteria vary, and they are commonly associated with transforming something into something else. Bacteria in the digestive system break down nutrients, such as complex sugars, into forms the body can use.[7] Certain types of bacteria get their energy through consuming organic carbon. Most absorb dead organic material. Other types of bacteria are considered hazardous and conduits of diseases.

Transmutation is the action of changing or the state of being changed into another form. In physics and chemistry, it means the changing of one element into another by radioactive decay, nuclear bombardment or similar processes. Esotericism applies a parallel idea to that of those sciences. Based on both schools, energy transmutation can be understood to occur when an energy pattern is reversed to its opposite aspect.[2]

Metaphysically, bacteria are transmutative beings. That is, the etheric energy that collectively envelops them transmutes the elements of the environment. Hence, wherever bacteria are observed in the body or in the house – either the so-called good bacteria found in the gut flora, or the hazardous ones in decaying flesh – there is the need to control stagnant or harmful emotions.

The etheric plasma that envelops bacteria vibrates at frequencies close to the purple frequencies in the colour spectrum. This indicates the end of a cycle and the beginning of another. Consequently, the bacteria which affect people and animals, either positively or negatively, absorb the etheric residues of organic or inorganic matter which are at the end of their lives.

The physical lives of cells are determined by a chemical state known as "equilibrium". Equilibrium is a stage in which chemicals no longer tend to react over time.[8] In biology, it is well known that the life of a cell is based on the chemicals that exchange energy to keep each other from reaching equilibrium, which prevents the cells from dying. Thus, bacteria will only appear when equilibrium is evident.

Essentially, bacteria absorb stagnant energy and exude the prospect of new life.

To eliminate harmful bacteria, such as the ones found in infections or wounds or the ones that cause food poisoning, the ignored emotions in these parts of the body must be healed. The healing should be accompanied by the understanding that an emotion in that part of the body was stagnant or corrupted, therefore at the end of its life.

Likewise, wishing for the ending of an emotion may result in unconsciously attracting bacteria to one's organisms or house, thus having the bacteria do the renovation work, reflecting an illness which is the somatisation of that emotion.

Insects are part of a collective system which is sustained by the imbalance of environments. They serve a noble purpose of balancing and stabilising environments, either in the wilderness or in people's homes.

Depending on the insect in question, the specific emotion in disharmony may be assessed:

Ants

Ants emanate an energetic plasma that simulates a pheromone of pleasure and sweetness. These waves radiating from ants or anthill strings in the house are a sign of where such a plasma is missing. In the same way that ants exhale this pheromone of sweetness, they absorb the antagonists of sweetness and pleasure, in this case, bitterness and lack of interest.

It is worth taking into consideration that, similarly to ants, most insects exhale and absorb such etheric particles and gases wherever they are, balancing emotionally affected environments. The use of insecticides does not solve the problem, quite the contrary, it evidences a disregard for life.

Simple attitudes may divert ants from the house. A neatly swept and organised home would suffice. Moreover, pots with flowers and cheerful pictures on the walls have a colossal impact on individuals' psyche. Fresh bedding and open windows are excellent to keep ants at bay. Lastly, broken objects should be discarded. Once the home is etherically "sweet", it will turn bitter for ants, which will in turn then leave.

Cockroaches

Cockroaches exude a semi-physical plasma of conservation while absorbing the etheric gases of disgust. Wherever a cockroach can be found, there resides a need for conservation, either physical or moral.

Therefore, these insects are a sign that self-preservation and self-protection are needed, as it is conspicuous that there is something the individual wishes to eliminate from their life.

The fact that cockroaches absorb the dense energies of the environment, such as those of aversion, indicates that these insects spontaneously act in the dissociation of etheric putrid gases.

Just as the elementals of nature filter the most subtle ethers, cockroaches filter the densest ethers. In this way, they involuntarily warn that extra care must be taken. These alerts are not exclusively for humans, but for other animals in the environment, who instinctively perceive them. Therefore, the intact nature is balanced with the help of all insects, animals and plants that are part of it.

The persistent killing of cockroaches will not solve the problem. On the contrary, others will appear to continue the motion of exuding and absorbing. Thus it is recommended that the individual affected by an infestation alter their low mental and emotional patterns to patterns of a higher frequency.

Acceptance of the space in which an individual lives is crucially necessary, as is the understanding that other individuals do not invade anyone's space, but, in fact, the individuals themselves unconsciously auto-project the judgement and disgust of the world.

Spiders

Spiders only appear at places where the energies of professional work are not being exercised. These may be stagnant thoughts of doubt, stunted ideals and undetectable desire to invest in a career. They may also denote mental or physical lethargy.

When spiders appear, they occupy the precise areas where that professional labour energy is scarcely found. Spiders absorb stagnation and exude etheric plasma similar to the planning of a work that requires physical or intellectual effort. Indubitably, owning a house in the countryside or an apartment on the 50th floor will be decisive for the appearance of spiders, nevertheless, the consciousness that inhabits a house in the woods and the consciousness that lives on the 50th floor of a skyscraper think rather differently from each other concerning professional success.

The spiders' webs will only be made on surfaces lacking professional energy; therefore, books covered in webs must be read; ceilings or walls camouflaged with them demand the repositioning of furniture or for the room to be redecorated.

In the case of a spider infestation, investing in a course or studies should be considered. Additionally, reading, planning and work from home ameliorate the circumstances.

In nature, spiders play a role in stimulating other insects and small port animals to physiologically develop survival skills.

Mice and rats

Mice, as well as rats, are animals already constituted with a fully structured astral body, however, they are still thoroughly connected to other nearby rats and mice spiritually, as if they were a group of a singular soul.

The energy that sustains rats and mice, varying in intensity between the two groups, is one of the most unstable in the animal world. Rats and mice are capable of feeling the frequency variations more sharply than the vast majority of animals, even more so than cats or dogs.

According to tales from mediaeval Europe, rats were seen as mediators from the underworld, considering that they are always under the houses' floors and on the earth.

Coincidentally, the etheric reality of rats does not diverge from this line of thought. Rats possess etheric energy that is constantly changing in frequency. They are animals that both interact with benevolent, organised and enlightened frequencies as well as with the densest, most chaotic and dark frequencies. These qualities can be observed from a purely physical point of view, as mice are found both in putrid manholes or in clean and airy rooms in houses, modern offices and spacious churches.

In the areas where etheric waves are conflictual, exhibiting a discrepancy of frequency, mice will appear. Although mice have extensive adaptive skills to dwell in different frequency layers, they are attracted to places where such frequency conflict is constant.

Incontestably, there are materialistic reasons why rats and mice would appear, which are key to determining such an occurrence in the physical world. However, metaphysical complementation offers the primary motivation why matter and physical beings behave in such ways. The materialistic reasons are based on observational agents, whereas a metaphysical explanation focuses on the astral factors behind reality as it is experienced.

As an example, the materialistic reasons why mice infest a house could be gaps in the walls or food crumbs on the floor. This, however, fails to explain why an individual would live in a house with gaps in the walls or why they would have floors covered with food crumbs.

In order to keep rats and mice away from home, the conflicting frequencies in the environment must be ceased. These conflicts in certain sites are generated by individuals whose emotional discrepancies are continual, for example, a person praying devoutly in the morning who later at night has an altercation at the same place. Or the individual who beautifully makes a bed while leaving the chest of drawers completely disorganised. Or even people who live in chaos at home, but are serene and organised on the street or at work, and vice versa.

These conflicting energies can be generated by either emotional or physical reasons, linked to habits. Rats and mice only appear when there is chaos and conflict generated by the individuals who spend considerable amounts of time in those places. Hence, rats and mice will not feel at ease in places with no variation of frequency, as they may feel maladjusted.

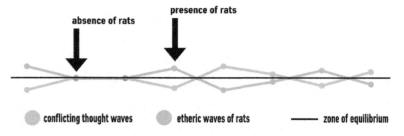

*Upon encountering a human's conflicting thoughts, the ethe-
ric waves of rats and mice involuntarily compensate for
the peaks and valleys, aiming for an equilibrium.*

The more calamitous or nefarious the energies, the more prone
to rats a place would be. The more superficial or flippant the
energies, the more prone to mice a place would be.

It is therefore not suggested that traps be used. Killing
rats to get rid of them is paradoxical, since these animals are
unconsciously attracted to repairing the energy imbalance
of the environment. In addition, the holes and gaps in the
walls must be sealed and all areas must be cleaned regularly.
Ultimately, positive thoughts, emotions and habits that are
aligned with each other must be cultivated.

Butterflies

Butterflies are surrounded by etheric currents which vibrate
at frequencies that closely resemble thought-forms. Therefore,
butterflies can be observed at places where thought-forms are
abundant, even in the wilderness.

Exteriorised thoughts are composed of a stream of subtle
particles and waves, whereas thought-forms are constituted
by the etheric solidification of much more complex thoughts.

Thought-forms are also the main conductor of the energy marks of a particular place, which was theorised as the "morphogenetic field".

Morphogenetic fields indicate that, biologically, all populations are informed by consciousness fields previously irradiated by other beings of the same species. A morphogenetic field is, therefore, a memory field that all species move through, think and behave correspondingly.[9]

Butterflies are enveloped in a frequency close to that of thought-forms, hence in certain circumstances, they will interact or behave according to them. That is, they may be influenced by the thought-forms of the environment, as well as influencing them.

Metaphysically, butterflies absorb the energies that spread in all directions simultaneously, while exhaling waves that redirect these thoughts. Depending on the energetic eminence of the thought-forms, it may be that a butterfly is naturally attracted near where the thought-form is, to experience more of that energy familiar to the species.

It is also important to emphasise that only in abnormal circumstances will butterflies interact with the thought-forms of humans, such as landing on a certain book, when there is an examination to be sat; or landing on a photo frame, while thinking deeply about who is in the image; or perhaps landing on top of the head at the time of prayer; or even landing on a bunch of keys, when a decision is made.

Insects of all types appear only when the etheric vibration of places makes this possible.

As discussed, insects are mainly governed by a collective etheric plasma. That is, a group of insects behaves and evolves as if they were part of an entire soul. This collective "soul" travels in the physical and semi-physical world, absorbing and exhaling ethers invisible to physical eyes. This indicates how each insect on Earth is needed to balance the type of frequency the planet is at.

It is advantageous to talk to the insects, in the case of an infestation. Communication is not properly done through words, but through the vibrational field of the human and the vibrational field of insects. As nature establishes the equilibrium of forces, the vibrational fields of both will attempt to achieve that balance. Consequently, both humans and insects will be urged to change, no longer needing each other's presence to achieve the equilibrium of forces in nature.

Ancestral and Psychical Composition

As mentioned, ants ooze a pheromone of sweetness. They are beings that have had their atmans detached from Source on the frequency range related to love, which includes other dealings such as kindness, diplomacy and harmonic beauty. These frequency bands are different frequencies of Source, and paralleling Source with a rainbow, each colour would vibrate in a different frequency and amplitude, red having the longest range, and violet the shortest.

Each of these vibrating sections, exemplified as colours of a rainbow, are different shades of the same Source or God. Hence, the seven basic frequencies can be denominated: Evolution; Generation; Justice; Love; Law; Knowledge; Faith.

Within these basic frequencies, others are also expressed as derivations of the initial frequencies. As examples: movement, which derives from Law; peace, which derives from Faith; work, which derives from Knowledge; kindness which derives from Love.

The ants' Atman holograms have come off the "region" of Source related to Love. And although ants had their atmans generated in the wave of Love, these beings had an extensive evolutionary journey until they finally became ants, as they were probably mineral plasma, unicellular beings and other insects before they became ants. All, commonly, were sustained in their evolution by the wave of Love.

It is pivotal to reiterate that the atmans of these insects are not paired with the number of insects in a colony. For example, a colony of 2800 ants does not mean 2800 atmans. Most likely, one Atman radiates to all ants in the colony. At the moment of migration to another realm, the Atman of the collectivity may split into other parts, though not necessarily into 2800 fragmented atmans, but possibly to just a few or even migrate as a lone Atman.

All animals, including insects, are beings that were generated by one of the specific waves of creation. Source creates all matter from distinct bands of frequency, which gives unique characteristics to each element created.

The creation of atmans, which are the essence of each animal and human, occurs comparably.

Assuming that ants could navigate across other realms while keeping their essence when turning into beings of another species, they would likely be rose quartz crystals if they entered the mineral kingdom. They would be roses or passion fruit flowers if they were to become part of the plantae kingdom. Along these lines, they would find themselves as chickens, peacocks, herons or storks if they were to initiate their lives in this class of animals.

Such compatibility is defined concerning the frequency from each of the aforementioned beings descended. The frequency of love notably associates ants, rose quartz, roses and chickens into a group that shares a spiritual gene of love within their atmans. All animals, including insects, are beings that were generated by one of the qualities of Source.

Although various bees are linked to honey, these insects have had their divine sparks detached from the waves of Generation, or more precisely, Motherhood. Their atmans emerged from the power of Divine Generation; however, each being in the universe acquires other frequency enhancements during their evolution, either as a collective group or as an individual. The Atman, or Divine spark, remains unaffected, although the capsules in the form of other bodies temporarily grant nuances of other Divine aspects. Thus, bees emerged from the frequency of Generation, simultaneously being supported by the frequency of Knowledge, or more explicitly, the frequencies of work and labour.

As collective spirits, which denotes the insects that, despite having a complex etheric body, are still behaving and gathering experience as if the group is one soul, the spiritual journey of bees commenced on the planet Venus. There, they were incarnated in a substantially more subtle plane than the third dimension experienced on Earth. Hence, life on Venus is categorically impossible for animals or plants of the Earth; however, not every spirit in the universe experiences "incarnation" in the physical third dimension, but in other dimensions too, either subtler or denser than that experienced on Earth.

Considering several animals with a pineal gland, more specifically cats, owls and horses, it is noticed that much of their behaviour is established by magnetic signals received by the antenna gland.

Horses

Horses are among the animals that have the most developed pineal gland, from an extra-physical point of view. Most horses have premonitions, a keen intuition and they may, in certain circumstances, witness disembodied spirits. Horses are also one of the closest spirits to migrate to a viable hominid realm.

Cats

Cats sleep most of the day because at night they filter out harmful energy from the environment. Physiologically, they save energy during the day, hence after sunset and before sunrise is the time when they are most active. This pattern demonstrates the compatibility between physiological and extra-physical behaviours.

The biological and instinctual reasons for such behaviour are acknowledged and taken into consideration, nevertheless, the approach to extra-physical argumentation is the primal reason why cats' physical bodies developed in this way.

The part of the house where cats lie is presumably the place where the most energetic attention is needed.

Cats' eyes are also powerful vortices of subtle energy, and their magnetism is not due merely to their physical attractiveness.

The electromagnetic field generated by the feline pineal gland, especially that of the domestic cat, is extraordinarily sensitive to the macrocosmic and interpersonal energies of their owners. Cats can detect energy shifts in the field networks, both from the environment and from other beings.

Additionally, their pineal glands can channel the frequency of thoughts of humans, therefore sensing whether those humans have an innocent or corrupt intention towards them.

In the etheric dimensions, they may perceive the regions where there is a lack of vital energy, hence they involuntarily commence a process of etheric filtration, where they sleep close to these areas to promote their revitalisation.

If the electromagnetic field of humans collides with the field of an individual they are in disharmony with, it may cause the annihilation of electrons and positrons in their own field.

The mutual annihilation creates polarised photons that may collide with other photons, thereby generating other harmful particles, (as opposed to generating anti-photons, since the photons have no charge or mass).

Under such circumstances, cats cleanse and demagnetise holographic antimatter in their owner's electromagnetic fields.

Cats are comparable to clear crystals, as they also stimulate mental clarity in their owners.

The more energetically imbalanced the house or the owner's aura, the more corrosive energy the cat may absorb, which perhaps leaves the cat prone to a compromised state of health.

Between 3:00 am and 4:30 am is the time when cats most transmute energy, as it is the part of the day when less vital energy flows in the environment. It is hence recommended that cats are allowed to sleep at any given time they require.

Appropriate attention should be given to the area where a cat chooses to sleep, ensuring its physical and energetic cleanliness.

Owls and eagles

Owls and eagles are related to night and day, respectively. That is, while the former's instincts will thrive at night-time, the latter's nature excels during the daytime.

Interestingly, owls have perfect night vision, while eagles have incredible eyesight during the day. The eyes of eagles are large compared to the size of their heads, as the posterior corner of their eyeball exhibits a flatter and larger back wall than that of humans' eyes. Such a contour permits them wider view angles.

The eyesight of eagles is five times more accurate than that of humans; moreover, they can perceive five basic colours, compared to three by humans. They can also detect ultraviolet light, which human eyes cannot.

Their astute capabilities resonate with their own astral aspects. In other words, eagles have such physical capabilities as a result of the divine nature of their essence.

These two birds carry a generous amount of apatite crystals in their pineal glands, which have their atoms' elementary particles strictly arranged in peculiar shapes, allowing the antenna gland to easily tune in to the subtle planes of the intellect.

The plane of the intellect, which is a distinct layer derived from other dimensions, allows knowledge and facts to be considered from different angles in synchronicity.

Both owls and eagles act their etheric energies on physical renewal and rebirth.

Eagles and owls are constantly renewing their physical bodies. When eagles see themselves as old and weak, they tear out their own feathers, to grow new and stronger ones. They also dismount their own beaks, and a much thicker and sharper one replaces the decayed one. The Egyptian myth of the phoenix originated from the observation of this phenomenon of physical rebirth. Upon dying, the bird was consumed by flames and then arose from its own ashes as a new phoenix.

Owls couple intellect with intuition. Their impeccable night vision and their non-physical bodies are highly efficient at comprehending what implicit events mean.

Pigeons, dolphins and whales

The sounds emitted by animals such as dolphins and pigeons drift into phonon waves, which are quasi-particles associated with sound, just as the photons are associated with light. Both pigeons and dolphins can balance entangled damaging etheric currents.

All sorts of pigeons act on the mental cleansing of egregores, which is the spiritual force created by the sum of the collective mental and emotional energies of a group. Pigeons, therefore, influence the respiratory energy of individuals as well as undoing group mental confusion, especially at places where there is considerable transit or influx of people.

Pigeons have a sense called magnetoreception, which allows them to detect a magnetic field to perceive direction, altitude or location. For these animals, magnetoreception deals with the detection of the Earth's magnetic field. Physiologically, their magnetic receptors allow them to navigate, which includes the ability, in homing pigeons, to return to their homes using the capacity to sense the Earth's magnetic field and other cues to orient themselves.[10, 11, 12]

Curiously, when assessing the more subtle properties of electromagnetism sensing, pigeons emit sounds in an attempt to share information on "what to do" or "where to go". This creates a sound chain that intercepts the crossing phonon waves of a particular place, dissipating mental nodes amid the species. The mental nodes of any humans nearby are also favourably influenced by the compassing sounds.

Dolphins use sound to detect the size, shape and speed of objects hundreds of metres away under water, which is nearly five times faster at conducting sound waves than air. This ability to use echo to determine the density of objects allows them to simply emit a sound to distinguish a ping-pong ball from a golf ball, by creating acoustic and 3D shapes in their heads and analysing their density. Moreover, they can sense if another animal is dead or alive, simply by sensing their pulsation echoing. These marine creatures use sonar as a sense, communicating with one another via clicks, whistles and trills.[13]

Metaphysically, the sounds of dolphins perform an involuntary cleansing on depressive emotions that are entangled. Their sounds dispel sadness in the emotional bodies of individuals, and the image of the trauma may also be dissipated by the dolphin itself, although the latter is performed secondarily, on rare occasions.

The echoing can trigger entangled and deeply anchored emotions in the subconscious, bringing them to the surface to finally be dismantled. The healing effects of listening to dolphin sounds is indeed a gradual and relatively slow process, nevertheless, it is effective as a side therapy for depressed individuals, those who may have lost a loved one and for those who struggle to find a purpose in life.

Several spiritual rescue groups have used such natural sounds to treat the spirits of depressive suicidal individuals, such is the healing power of that vibration. Rescue teams which are organised by enlightened spirits, generally need an ever so slightly denser form of energy when conducting cases where the patient is still profoundly attached to earthly conditioning. Thus, these teams gather the rescued individuals to accompany them to areas of the sea where there are many dolphins, whose sounds and vibrations help dissipate the agonies and traumas of the afflicted.

Pigeons are animals of the air, whereas dolphins live in water. This difference characterises pigeons as healers of the mind, while dolphins are the healers of emotions.

In other dimensions, the sounds emitted by dolphins reverberate inside the object or throughout the individual's subtle bodies, hence the dolphin may recognise what sort of emotional "filling" is there. Those echo back to their minds, thus being dispelled for simply looking unfavourable, as in entangled traumas.

The sounds of whales refer to feminine polarity vibrations capable of defragmenting unconscious traumas related to guilt, fear and shame, thus enabling these destructive emotions to be assessed and healed. It is no coincidence that numerous cultures indicate the relationship between whales and oceans with the subconscious mind.

In the Old Testament there is a narrative[14] where Jonah disobeys the orders of God and, as a consequence, the man immediately becomes depressed and distressed for not following what the creator had asked him to do.

Then, on being thrown into the sea, Jonah was swallowed by a whale (or 'big fish'), staying three days in the animal's belly. Jonas says the three days were pure fear, as he was in the most abysmal place in the world. However, when he asked for forgiveness, God ordered the big fish to vomit Jonah.[15]

Coincidence or not, the astral implications of whale sounds are directly connected to overcoming traumas and guilt.

Perhaps when these animals spiritually evolve to a more intellectual realm they may possess the ability to helping the emotionally traumatised.

The sounds emitted by whales unconsciously lead listeners to slow down their breathing, which aids in relieving anxiety episodes. Metaphysically, these healing sounds are interpreted as maternal, non-threatening sounds, which gently agitates the depths of one's lower mental body's crystallised traumas that might have developed throughout upbringing. This results in a sedative sensation, thereby ameliorating the processes of eliminating such agonies. It is worth noting that these sounds, recorded on digital devices, can be used in the treatment of animals victimised by trauma and physical shock.

Bats

Despite being extensively linked to witchcraft, legends of vampires and general evil, bats are a group of animals that, metaphysically, are identified with dissipating mental stagnation. Circumstantially associated with the macabre, both bats and spiders are beings who act where and when the lack of vigorous mental activity is perceptible.

Both animals are correlated with the qualities of the element air, which transpires intellect, thoughts, imagination and ideas. Spiders, however, are conduits of intellectualised labour, whereas bats are conduits of intellectualised courage, that is, courage based on evidence and facts.

Bats are also known for their impressive echolocation capability, which resembles that of dolphins and pigeons.[16] Bat's echolocation, however, calls range in frequency from 14,000 to over 100,000 Hz. Bats emit much longer signals than dolphins, as well as more varied ones.

These nocturnal animals interpret data much quicker than most species with echolocation, which grants them the power to simultaneously act on several different targets.

This natural etheric trait of bats is beneficial to those afraid of taking action, including all mammals. Hence a stroll in a dark forest may dismantle more fears than just that of the dark forest itself.

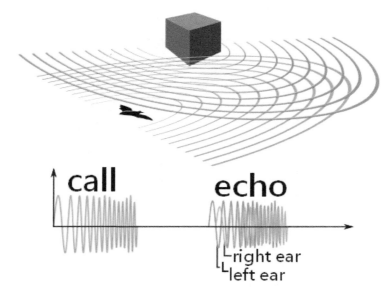

A representation of a bat, its ultrasound call and the echo from an object. Credit: Petteri Aimonen

Antagonistically, the archetype of bats has been metamorphosed to less beneficial nuances, such was the correlation between these creatures with evil and dark forces throughout the centuries, in virtually all cultures. Thus, it is recommended to understand that bats, like spiders, are divine principles in evolution, which have nothing to do with harmful magic or any demonological connotation.

Sparrows and canaries

Birds such as sparrows are sensitive to signals from mental currents. They adapt to these subtle signals, behaving differently through the quality of the thought-forms of humans and other mammals.

Similar to sparrows, canaries are sensitive to mental images, although they may sing more than the former.

Both sorts of birds, as well as budgies, lovebirds and cockatiels, do not sing as a result of thought-forms or as a warning or supernatural hypothesising. Nevertheless, the abnormal behaviour of an unknown wild animal may determine the possibility of friendly spirits attempting to communicate, although these occurrences are exceptionally rare.

In metaphysics, sparrows stimulate focus, not only in humans but in other animals too. It is convenient to remember that all animal extra-physical activity has distinct effects on both humans and other animals.

Canaries denote favourable ideas, unravelling conflicting thoughts. In the wild, canaries boost local mental activity, regardless of the presence of humans. Mental activity, therefore, should not be understood as an exclusively human faculty.

Dogs and cats

Dogs have a tremendous capacity for loving unconditionally.

The centre of a dog's electromagnetic field is one of the largest in the animal kingdom, thus the purification of degrading and depressing emotions in the environment are efficiently dispersed by the strong currents coming from the canine heart chakras. Their powerful vortex influences humans on the grounds of interpersonal energies. Dogs are among a limited number of animals able to cause such repercussions, invariably nourishing to the etheric bodies of humans. This influence occurs as the dogs "soften the individuals' hearts" by dissolving resentments while pleasantly filling energy gaps caused by the rigidity of adult life.

Although granted intellectual traits, dogs are primarily developing emotional skills in their incarnations.

Dogs are uncommonly synergetic, that is, they smell energy and may even see it in some cases. They prudently distinguish positive energy from malefic energy, hence they regularly sleep in the cleanest areas in the house, unless told not to do so.

Metaphysically, hair or fur relates to one's superiors – one's power figure, owner or boss. If envious forces are projected against an individual, the dog may develop hair problems, as an involuntary mechanism of protecting the human they honour.

In spite of what some may assume, dogs are neither foolish nor empty-headed for repeatedly "coming back wagging their tails" to those who were cruel to them. This is due to their ability to easily forgive. In such a way, dogs involuntarily help humans to learn to forgive, reflecting purity in its highest degree. Their astral bodies are fully formed, but still, they will not hold indignation or wrath against others, for the reason, they do not need to redeem karma debts, only learn new experiences.

The non-physical version of the dog's thymus gland, which is the subtle centre of love, next to the heart, works energetically identical to the thymus glands found in humans.

Dogs expand benevolent energies, whereas cats transmute malefic ones. The reason why cats transmute and dogs expand energies is due to the direction in which their electromagnetic currents move. The electromagnetic field of cats is centripetal, while that of the dog is centrifugal. This means that cats absorb the negative energy, transmute it within themselves and thereupon return it to the environment. Dogs, alternatively, generate positive energy within themselves, redistributing it.

The reason why cats will not absorb every single type of energy except the harmful ones is plainly due to the frequency in which the energies vibrate. Cats' electromagnetic fields, which are negative in polarisation, will only interlace with positive currents, that is, the environment's negative energies. They hence "drag" these sorts of energy to the centre of their electromagnetic field, where transmutation occurs. The transmutation performed by a cat is a process where particles and waves are spun to the opposite direction of natural spin.

Dogs, on the other hand, have their fields performing in an expansive, i.e. centrifugal way, therefore they do not draw energy, as the movement is naturally from the inside out. However, dogs become emotionally attached to their owners and, as a consequence, they feel and connect to their aura. As such, these animals may somatise in themselves energetic imbalances from the human. Somatisation, in this case, is the surge of diseases in the physical body due to imbalances found in the most subtle bodies, such as the etheric and the astral bodies.

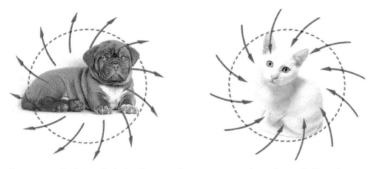

Dogs exude beneficial ethers, whereas cats absorb malefic ethers.

Domesticated animals commonly radiate more beneficial ethers than the humans they share the house with, as they normally lack negative thoughts and malicious behaviour. As a consequence, episodes of energetic compensation may occur when they involuntarily donate their energies to the human auric fields, hence developing the very diseases meant to afflict the human.

Finally, the energy of all animals, either small insects or intelligent mammals, will inevitably interact with the energies of other animals and of humans. Mediumistic abilities in humans may also be nothing but fundamental characteristics inherent in several animals.

SPIRITUAL REPERCUSSIONS OF EATING MEAT

The spiritual and energetic repercussions of eating meat must be understood as the reaction one's subtle body displays after the ingestion of meat or other etherically toxic foods of animal origin.

The following chapter will exclusively discuss meat. However, some of the concepts discussed here may be applied to other foods and by-products or services resulting from animal exploitation, such as the use of skins and furs, feathers and bones.

The totality of the human being, as an incarnated spirit, is composed of seven main bodies. They are the Physical; the Etheric; the Astral; the Lower Mental; the Upper Mental; the Buddhic; and the Atman body. Through some of these bodies and meridians, different types of energy are distributed. Meridians carry *qi/chi* or *prana* from and to the physical body. These energy canals also conduct other categories of energy that travel through the physical organs, tissues and liquids to and from the etheric body and the astral body. They are the macrocosmic energy; ancestral energy; respiratory energy; food energy; and interpersonal energy.

With reference to the aforementioned bodies and types of energy, meat is to be assessed for its etheric components, as well as "where" and "how" these energies reverberate in the human body.

Meat and Antimatter

As well as having a physical body, animals are endowed with an etheric body which provides them with energy at the same time as it serves as a glue between their physical bodies and their astral bodies. Their astral bodies, like the humans', is the duplicate of the physical body in the astral dimension.

The emotions of sentient beings are typically stored in their astral bodies. When negative, these emotions are carriers of antimatter in the subtle planes.

Antimatter is one of the main components of the commonly named "negative energy". A particle of matter and a particle of antimatter both have the same mass, but the electrical charge of antimatter is generally opposite to that of ordinary matter, as exemplified in the case of the electron and positron or the proton and antiproton.[1]

A clairvoyant medium can observe antimatter in the aura of individuals, either as a particle or as a wave. These peculiar reversed particles in the aura signify for the individual an energetic deficiency caused by the stagnation of vital flow and the accumulation of astral detritus.

Naturally, the physical body is composed of matter, however, the etheric body is constituted of subtle matter, which can be understood as regular matter, but natural to another dimension.

All in the physical dimension is composed of matter, made up of electrons, quarks and other elementary particles. Every particle (and antiparticle) is fundamentally an excitation in all-permeating quantum fields.

When particles and antiparticles meet, they annihilate each other. Nevertheless, the energy resulting from mutual destruction must go somewhere. Thus, photons with high energy are propelled, giving rise to various proportions of gamma rays and neutrinos. Most of the total energy of annihilation emerges in the form of ionising radiation, which consists of subatomic particles or electromagnetic waves that have sufficient energy to ionise atoms or molecules by detaching electrons from them. As a result, that two-way liquidation reduces the size of the electromagnetic field of molecules and atoms.

If the surrounding subtle matter, or holographic matter, is present during annihilation, the energy content of this radiation will be absorbed and converted into other forms of energy, such as destructive heat or light. The amount of energy released is usually proportional to the total mass of the collided matter and antimatter, in accordance with the notable mass-energy equivalence equation, $E = mc^2$.

All in all, subtle antimatter annihilates subtle matter, which reflects on the illness of the etheric body and, consequently, negatively affects the physical body. It is also crucial to emphasise that the matter and antimatter found in the subtle bodies are holographic particles, that is, they are still to gain mass and become completely physical.

Wave-particle duality is the concept of quantum mechanics that says that every particle or quantum body can be described as either a particle or a wave, depending on how it is observed and measured.[2] Thus, along with the ingestion of meat, there is the unavoidable ingestion of its electromagnetic wave, which contains information on how that flesh was generated. The information is presented as distortions caused by antimatter, which disfigure the wave frequency patterns. As the eaten meat becomes part of the physical body, the electromagnetic wave that constitutes it will become part of the individual's electromagnetic field.

By attracting antimatter to its own etheric body through ingestion, the individual causes the destruction of matter as well as the destruction of the attracted antimatter, that is, they annihilate each other, causing loss of vital fluids in the region and in the entire physical body. This mutual annihilation leads to the release and loss of photons and neutrinos in the etheric body. Therefore, lacking a natural flow of vital energy, the physical body will present epigenetic and emotional abnormalities.

In a similar vein, the consumption of antimatter found in meat in the form of waves perforates the etheric body of those who consume it, since antimatter annihilates matter which is still in its etheric form as a hologram. Etheric matter, or ethereal matter, is matter in its embryonic stage. It commonly condenses as physical matter, to make part of one's physical body.

All in all, antimatter invariably appears on the subtle bodies before manifesting in the physical body.

Although it is presumed that meat may offer one of the five types of subtle energy, it is imperative to indicate that the molecular and atomic constitution of food also manifests the quality of energy being transmitted and absorbed, not just its calories.

The pains that an animal experience at the very moment of death, or the panic that precedes it, leave scarring marks on their etheric bodies. The etheric body is the subtle body that vitalises the physical body with vital fluids. This means that these dreadful feelings, which reside at low vibration frequencies, consequently permeate the animal's flesh, as well as the rest of their physical bodies.

In these circumstances, there is no "energy cleansing" that could potentially liberate the meat from such energies, since the physical molecules of the meat have been generated or redefined at a molecular level, under such low frequencies.

The terror and pain during their deaths are not the only moments that affect their physical bodies on this level. Confinement and incapability of expressing their natural instincts also influence their subtle bodies, including the lower and upper mental bodies. Calves that are taken from their mothers seconds after birth; chickens that never enjoy spreading their wings; pigs that will never touch the natural ground or see a ray of sunlight during their lives; all this suffering[3] contributes to shaping how each molecule of their meats will be generated at the subatomic level.

Elementars are static beings shaped by the repeated emotions of incarnated sentient beings. They are the result of beliefs and thoughts sustained by strong emotions. The elementars are intensified holograms, which have no life of their own, but they appear to exercise some function in the astral world. Under constant terror, animals will involuntarily fabricate elementars, which will remain connected to their physical bodies and, consequently, to their flesh.

"Elementars" and "elementals" are different characters. Elementars are energies shaped in the astral dimension, whereas elementals are, in most cases, prototypes of the souls of animals or other beings who dwell in certain vibrational bands of the elements of nature, such as fire, air, water and earth.

The vast majority of animals lined up to be slaughtered create a form of holographic shield around themselves, as a means of protection. Unfortunately, this shield is nothing more than a holographic projection of their energies. These shields are described as elementars.

Upon being killed, the astral bodies of those animals separate from their elementars. However, their corpses still retain attachments to those holograms. Generally, elementars' shields produced in life act as a toxic layer over those who produce them, which would serve to avert the enemy. When eating meat, the possibility of consuming its allocated elementars is considerable.

Psychosomatic Complications

Upon eating meat, the transfer of vital fluids from subtle bodies to the physical body is reduced, as a result of blockages caused by the low amplitude of frequency in the meat, which prevents energy in the subtle body from moving smoothly.

The emotional body of an individual who has eaten meat will naturally assimilate the feelings attached to the meat, which may motivate psychosomatic illnesses, which occur when the mind and emotions generate a physical disease in the body itself, in a forced activity to purge it.

The animal's feelings attached to the flesh could be classified by the amount of accumulated antimatter in it, in addition to other particles derived from their thought-forms and elementars.

The solar plexus, also called celiac plexus, is not a chakra, but a physiological area in the human body. It is called solar plexus due to its radiating nerves, which resemble the sun. It is connected to several nerves and veins, besides being the locality in the human body with most nerves, after the brain.

The plexus is formed in part by the greater and lesser splanchnic nerves of both sides, and fibres from the anterior and posterior vagal trunks.

The celiac plexus proper consists of the celiac ganglia (neural structure) with a network of interconnecting fibres. The aorticorenal ganglia are often considered to be part of the celiac ganglia, and thus, part of the plexus.[4] It is over the solar plexus that the navel chakra, or *manipura,* is situated.

The solar plexus's etheric energy fundamentally exists to provide humans with an etheric shield, as well as functioning as a natural antenna, so better perception from the environment can occur. However, after eating meat, a considerable amount of etheric energy from that energy vortex is redirected to aid digestion.

Therefore, the individual's aura is momentarily compromised by the lack of etheric energy, which leaves it noticeably dispersed and subject to alien energies. For this reason, among others, various spiritual workers and mediums abstain from eating meat on the days when they should work with their subtle energies.

Humans have approximately 30 trillion cells in their body,[5] and within each cell there is a prototype system fairly similar to other large systems that comprise the human body in its entirety: a respiratory system, a digestive system, an excretory system, an endocrine system, a nervous system, a reproductive system and an immune system, as well as a nucleus, in which the entire genetic code is found.

In cell biology, it was believed that the nucleus of the cell would be associated with its "brain", an organ responsible for dictating how and when any voluntary or involuntary task is to be performed. This is still the case, as cells need a nucleus to divide themselves in order to replicate.

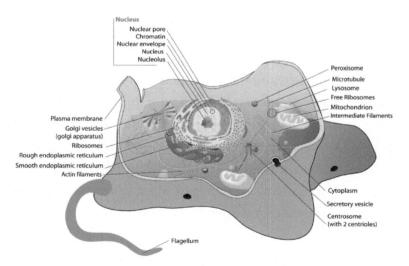

Structure of a typical eukaryotic cell (cell with a nucleus). Credit: Mariana Ruiz

Nevertheless, it was discovered[6] that the cells continued to live for approximately 60 days and still performed most tasks after they had their nuclei removed. For this reason, the nucleus is not the only system to control the cell, though it remains their primary control source.

Research also concluded that the membranes of cells were able to read external signals from the environment and, therefore, they were able to send these signals to proteins, telling them what to do. Thus. the membrane, not just the nucleus, played a role in telling proteins how to behave.

The signals perceived by the cell's membrane are of electric, chemical and electromagnetic nature. They are commonly associated with emotions, being transported by, but not limited to, neuropeptides and blood plasma.

Whenever a thought occurs, biological reactions follow, which indicates physical feedback. This implies that thoughts, via electrical and chemical derivatives, generate physical events. In these lines, it is understood that the mind influences the brain at the pace that the brain influences the mind.

Research explains the action of thoughts on organic cells:[6] whenever a thought occurs, an emotion follows. The emotion, physiologically perceived, is generated by neurotransmitters in the synapses.

The research has found that in the hypothalamus, these neurotransmitters join small chains of amino acids, producing neuropeptides. These neuropeptides act as activating hormones that spread through the blood. Once all cells have receptors for this neural chemistry, the peptides bind to the cell membrane, activating or deactivating genetic activity.

Subsequently, the cells' behaviour changes based on the quality of the neuropeptide. This is a phenomenon called epigenetics. Such a mechanism affects how cells work, altering the production of protein, changing inflammatory response and modulating immunological behaviour.

Thoughts that start as immaterial occurrences become material circumstances in the body, and likewise, cerebral automatism generates an idea, and that is reflected organically.

In conclusion, the cell's response to the environment is critically dependent on both its nucleus along with what its membrane may perceive in its environment. This determines that cells do behave and consequently may mutate as a result of their physiologic surroundings, regardless of what their DNA may carry.

Correlatively, the pain and emotions that animals experience during their lives may impact the behaviour and development of their cells, which certainly includes their flesh.

All matter has a holographic counterpart in the astral realm, that is, its exact copy called "etheric double".

When the individual lives in chaos, being surrounded by wrinkled clothes on the floor and dirty bed linen, the attraction of more astral chaos occurs, which may inevitably drift to the vicinity's physical dimension. The same assumption is taken with regard to accumulated dust and the general rubbish that agglomerates. Nevertheless, it is in the fridge and cupboards where such putrid condensation may allure the most chaotic varieties of astral waste.

Foods that are bought but not eaten, and that expire and rot, will generate a decaying quality of gases that spread onto other foods and in the corners of the rooms. These etheric gases block the flow of energy, causing mould, infiltration and insect infestations. This may even affect money flow and general health.

Even though they may be stored in the freezer or in vacuum-sealed tins, or even approach expiry date, meats in the cupboard and fridge go through a purification process in the etheric dimensions, which emit a sort of deep taupe colour fume, typically associated with astral worms. Animal fur and leather also undergo etheric putrefaction. Once in contact with the individual who wears it, the material may absorb, albeit moderately, some of the wearer's auric particles to etherically decompose in its totality.

Etheric Generation of Flesh

In quantum field theory, the quantum vacuum state is the quantum state with the lowest possible energy. Generally, this field does not contain physical particles either. However, it is by no means a simple empty space. According to quantum mechanics, the vacuum state is not truly empty but instead contains fleeting electromagnetic waves and particles that continually emerge and disappear from existence.[7]

The Higgs field, which is a quantum field, is a field of energy that is thought to exist in every region of the physical universe. The field is accompanied by a fundamental particle known as the Higgs boson, which is used by the field to continuously interact with other particles, such as the electron.

Particles that interact with the Higgs field gain mass from it, resulting in the slowing down of the particle, which also loses the ability to travel at the speed of light. If the Higgs field did not exist, particles would not have the mass required to attract one another, therefore they would float freely while their particle form remains travelling at light speed. Additionally, gravity would not exist, as mass would not exist to attract other mass. In other words, without the Higgs field there would only be light.[7]

"Giving mass" to an object is hence referred to as the Higgs effect. This effect transfers mass or energy to any particle that passes through the Higgs field. However, light that passes through it gains energy, but not mass, as its waveform does not have mass, while its particle form constantly travels at light speed.

The Higgs bosons contain the relative mass in the form of energy and, once the field has endowed a formerly massless particle, the particle in question will slow down and become "heavy", which may be understood as "materialised".

It is generally accepted that there is only one field in the universe, called the "electromagnetic quantum vacuum"; however, other fields are accepted to be parts of it, such as the Higgs field and the gravitational field. In this context, the Higgs field is the field related to matter, while the electromagnetic quantum vacuum is related to all physical creation.[8]

To understand such theories, the pattern of information that creates massless particles should be assessed.

In particle physics, the two known massless particles are the gauge bosons, i.e. the photon (carrier of electromagnetism) and the gluon (carrier of the strong force).

Elementary particles, whose interactions are described by the gauge theory, interact with each other by the exchange of gauge bosons, usually as virtual particles. All known gauge bosons have a spin of one; for comparison, the Higgs boson has spin zero. Therefore, all known gauge bosons are vector bosons.[9]

These virtual particles are created by the perturbation of a quantum field, which is described by the "perturbation theory" in quantum field theory. In a nutshell, a perturbation occurs when a specific locale of a quantum field changes its frequency or excitation, thus creating a particle from "nothing". The "nothing" is, in fact, an oscillation of a quantum field locale, as described by the perturbation theory.

In sacred geometry, it is understood that creation develops from geometrical structures, which can be holograms in the third dimension, albeit a fully formed object or entity in a much more subtle dimension.

The information contained in the waves of creation expresses itself into geometric shapes, known by some cultures today as God's geometry.[10]

Apart from being created by holographic geometric shapes, particles are also categorised in a concept of quantum mechanics called wave-particle duality, which states that every particle or quantum entity may be described as either a particle or a wave.

In the notion of particle-wave duality, it is hence accepted that upon eating food, the physical body will absorb the particle, while the etheric body will absorb the wave and, consequently, its information in the form of geometric holograms.

Equally, the information that was passed on to the flesh through the animals' etheric bodies are casualties of the environment and of their own feelings, but the information that generated every atom of their meat will also be absorbed as information by whomever eats it.

In metaphysics, meat is created by astral factors intended to help the spirit express its potentials in matter. The first molecules to become flesh in a living body are designed to strengthen intention, impede obstacles and guarantee courage. Literally, the reason why flesh, i.e. muscle, exists is to enable willpower to manifest in the third dimension. The muscles in animals, as well as in humans, have this physiological task: to guarantee the force of intention and action in matter. The greater is someone's muscle mass, without the need for physical exercise or dietary supplements, the greater is their strength of intention.

When the muscle is forcibly removed from the animal, that is, when the animal's force of intention is "used" by someone other than the owner of that muscle, that force (muscle) etherically becomes its anti-version, by having its polarities changed. Flesh, therefore, turns into an 'apathetic and pessimistic' matter. The geometry that initially formed those elementary particles from a quantum state, as a result, spins all of its holograms in their opposite directions. Such movement is not creative, which means that the piece of meat will not physically metamorphose into a different physical element, although its etheric version will.

Reasonably, questions may arise with regard to carnivorous animals in nature. However, the etheric life cycle of those animal's molecules of meat and tissues ends at the moment an animal kills the other. This is determined by the habitat's morphogenetic programming system.[11] In addition, the muscle and organs of animals are used in accordance with their natural needs before and during their physical deaths, as opposed to adapting to the artificial arrangements developed by animal husbandry.

BEHIND ANIMAL SACRIFICE

Animal sacrifice is the offering of an animal's life in a ritualistic ceremony.

Sacrificial slaughter has been present in numerous religions across the world, since ancient times, from the Hebrews, Greeks, Romans, Egyptians, Aztecs and Yoruba, to various contemporary cults.

The rituals in which animals are sacrificed often endeavour to appease a specific entity, god or even thank nature and the divine for what has been given. The ultimate purpose of a sacrifice is to supply a supernatural being with elements, thereupon the desire can be granted.

Religious slaughter first appeared parallel to the early civilisations in the Near East, with the oldest Egyptian burial sites containing animal remains originating from the Badari culture, which flourished between 4400 and 4000 BCE.[1]

According to scholars,[2] religious sacrifices may have derived from hunting practices, where hunters, feeling guilty for killing an animal, would try to mitigate their responsibility in these rituals, making their gods part of it and, therefore, being relieved of culpability. According to this theory, the hunters would also ease their consciences by suggesting that everybody should participate in the killing of the sacrificial victim. These justifying practices were especially identified in ancient Greece and Rome.

After the introduction of ritualistic animal slaughter, countless religions adopted the practice for the sole act of propitiation or worship, to incur divine favour or avoid divine retribution.

Different doctrines promoting animal sacrifice affirm that their deities would normally require specific victims related to their nature. For instance, the Roman gods of the "upper heavens" required white, infertile animals of their own sex: Juno a white heifer (possibly a white cow); Jupiter a white, castrated ox for the annual oath-taking by the consuls. Superior Gods with strong connections to the earth, such as Mars, Janus and Neptune, were offered fertile victims.[3]

In Western African cults, such as seen in the Yoruba cultures and African diaspora religions, each deity would be offered their favourite animal. Animals would also be sacrificed in rituals not aimed to please a deity, but to heal a disease, where a priest and other entities would transfer the individual's disease to the animal, who after being killed would take the disease with it. Other ritualistic slaughter includes the promotion of prosperity and the breaking of malignant spells.

Animal sacrifice is also a part of *Durga puja* celebrations during the Navratri in the eastern states of India. In the ritual, the goddess is offered a sacrificial animal in the belief that it stimulates her violent vengeance against the buffalo demon.[4] Nevertheless, these sacrifices are rare and most of them have usually been substituted by vegetarian offerings.

Although it is often assumed that ancient cultures may have offered animal sacrifices for nature to change its course, it is important to consider that, in those religions, every aspect of nature had one or multiple deities as their creators and rulers. For instance, in the old Aztec religion, Tlaloc is the god of rain; in the old Scandinavian religion, Njord is the god of the sea; and in Persian Zoroastrianism, Vayu-Vata are two gods often paired together; the former is the god of wind and the latter is the god of the atmosphere and air. Thus, a sacrificed offering aimed at changing the course of nature must be assumed as an offering to nature's governors.

In modern days, the term 'witchcraft' has acquired different connotations, symbolising both the classical malevolent conjurer or even individuals involved with the New Age movement. Nevertheless, witchcraft rituals associated with animal sacrifices are commonly those known as Black Magic, which can be identified in different cultures and periods of history, regardless of location or its devotees' racial backgrounds.

Therefore "Black Magic", in this case, refers to magic in the absence of light, and not to any Afro cultures, ethnicities or religions.

Black Magic, or "low magic", is normally understood as the counterpart of White Magic, or "high magic". The origins of Black Magic can be traced to the primitive worship of spirits in various populations.[5]

Unlike White Magic, which has traditionally been referred to as the use of supernatural powers or magic for selfless purposes, Black Magic is a primitive shamanistic effort to achieve closeness with spiritual beings in order to receive selfish outcomes.

An extensive parallel between animal slaughter in Black Magic and in ancient and modern cults is that ritualistic sacrifices of animals (and humans) are invariably assisted by discarnate spirits of people.

In a ritual where something is offered to an entity, the aura between the offerer and the entity is embedded in a phenomenon known as quantum entanglement. Thus, the offerer's intention allows the offering to be assigned to that specific entity, preventing any third party from potentially seizing the offering for themselves.

During a ritualistic offering where there is no slaughter, chants, candles, incense, symbols and hymns may be used so that the etheric double of the elements offered can be displaced, absorbed or utilised by the offered entity.

Contrary to popular belief, spirits given offerings neither eat nor drink the offerings. They normally manipulate the halo-energy of the offered elements, whereby they energetically fabricate the offerer's request into a sort of thought-form.

In most cases, when placing a request, the offerer generates a thought-form. Following this, the spirit being addressed magnetises that hologram with the manipulated energies that were obtained from the elements present in the offering. As the thought-form gains energy and magnetism, it spontaneously starts to attract future probabilities of what was initially requested.[6]

It is crucial to emphasise that ordinary discarnate spirits do not have the ability to manipulate the elements of an offering, should any be given to them. Therefore, spirits must normally master the art of energy manipulation between the dimensions, before being able to receive an offering. As for ordinary spirits, that is, spirits of discarnate individuals who do not play a role in religious or spiritualistic practices, the only way they can absorb energies from the physical third dimension is by the agency of energy *vampirisation* from a living person or animal.

When the offering consists of an animal's life, entities would typically absorb the etheric body of the animal upon slaughter. The dead physical body is of no use to the entity, and the animal's astral body normally "leaves" the scene, escorted by benevolent rescuers or attracted by immediate reincarnation.

Often, the animals sacrificed in religious ceremonies are those who possess, at least, an astral body, which is the replica of the physical body (or its matrix). In between the animal's astral and physical bodies lie the etheric body. The etheric body functions as the intermediate layer of the astral and physical bodies, serving to animate the physical body with more subtle aspects of the spirit as well as passing to the astral body all the repercussions of physical interaction and experiences. In the etheric body, the currents of *qi/chi*, prana or "life force" travel by the virtue of chakras – the energy vortices.

The etheric body consists of several layers of what is known as vital energy; however, most of it is in the form of ectoplasm.

Ectoplasm is a semi-physical gas, often characterised as a gelatinous, albeit extremely subtle fluid. All animals have ectoplasm, which is substantially produced by the physical body and, to some extent, by the astral body.

This fluid is exceptionally powerful, as it serves to not only invigorate physical bodies but also to potentiate the fabrication of objects in the astral realms. More importantly, it may give discarnate spirits, both the ordinary and the powerful malignant ones, the physical sensations experienced in the material world, as well as energy to reign, dominate and protect themselves in the lower zones of reality.

Countless maladjusted and malignant consciences flock to slaughterhouses in search of ectoplasm and the remains of the etheric bodies of slaughtered animals. Not only does the unfortunate vibration of those who suffer there serve to fuel the wrath of some vengeful spirits, their energetic remains are a powerful tool for such wicked disincarnates.

The holographic creation of mental images of animals about to die are mainly related to fear. These images are used by some spirits who, when introducing their vengeful and controlling spells into the physical world, exert great influence on wars and epidemics. Similarly, other vampire spirits, who were possibly bloodthirsty psychopaths in their past lives, use the remaining etheric bodies of slaughtered animals to feed themselves and thus experience carnal sensations. Many other spirits extremely attached to the vices of doing evil also gather in the corridors of the slaughterhouses, rejoicing in the midst of the semi-physical energies of so numerous corpses.

During the ritualistic slaughter, the animal's etheric body is not conserved into the shape of a body, but as a mist that would otherwise be absorbed by the etheric fields if not promptly abducted by an entity.

The spirits who would demand animal slaughter are generally malignant spirits, since low magic is related to selfish reasons which disregard the lives and the pain of others, in this case, those of sacrificed animals.

In sacrifices with animal slaughter, entities normally abduct the remains of the victim's etheric body.

In sacrifices without animal slaughter, entities manipulate the etheric-double of the elements offered.

The word "sacrifice" may signify either a sacred slaughter or the sacred offering of anything, such as food, libations or objects.

In several healing practices involving animal sacrifice, there are magic rituals that allegedly pass one's illness to the energetic body of an animal, which once dead, is presumed to take the disease with it.

Admittedly, the afflicted individual will experience a relative amelioration of their condition, however, the technique of "body-swapping" is constructed on a misinterpretation of what occurs in reality.

Initially, the ritual coalesces the external layers of the aura of both the human and the animal, where the maladies of the first are shared with the latter.

Subsequently, the animal's etheric body, which is absorbed by the entity, will serve to invigorate the magical spirit. From then on, this entity would reserve a certain amount of ectoplasm to produce kinds of etheric adhesives and binders to be applied to the individual's own etheric body. However, as the illness is generated in the astral body, the amelioration of symptoms is temporary. Therefore, the result of "body exchange" is of limited efficacy.

As observed in numerous religions and cults, the practice of making offerings for gods, nature and spirits is common. In certain faiths, the offering may include cuts of meat from an animal who was not ritualistically slaughtered.

However, the meats placed on an offering do not possess ectoplasm. However, as they are still physical elements, they do have a non-physical counterpart. Therefore, the elements of the offering are used to mould thought-forms or create holograms of future probabilities.

The subtle counterpart of meat is dense in its constitution. This means that the meat's etheric elements will assuredly be used to produce densified objects. Among these diabolical objects are the elementars and energetic strings that connect individuals in "love binding" spells.

In cults where pieces of meat are used in spiritual cleansing rituals, it is believed that the dense energies of someone or somewhere would be directed to the flesh, as spiritual entities assist such manoeuvring of energies. Although meat is not a highly recommended cleansing tool, since it etherically decomposes and pollutes, this kind of ritual is the closest to veracity regarding what really occurs in the invisible realms.

The utilised piece of meat is undoubtedly discarded after the ritual, and in its natural decaying process the malefic energies attached thereto are understood to be transmuted and reabsorbed into the streams of ether.

The entities responsible for the cleansing will normally be prepared to handle the pernicious elements, to avoid morbidities caused by meat's own negative aura. Nevertheless, most sects adept at this practice are not aware that, frequently, the entities behind requests for raw meat may have dubious intentions.

Religions that sacrifice animals may argue that the "energy" of the animal would go to the gods, however, this argument is strongly camouflaged by their exceedingly dogmatic rituals, sacrificial regalia and archaic fundamentals.

Despite the dismay some could feel towards these practices, the sacrifice of animals for occult purposes differs little from slaughtering animals for food.

ANIMAL WORSHIP IN ANCIENT RELIGIONS

Most ancient religions, especially those that thrived in ancient civilisations, were associated with animal adoration. In some cultures, animals were said to be symbols of the gods, in others, the animals personified the gods themselves. Numerous animals became mystical models, as in lucky pets, while others were said to bring bad luck or foreboding. The general evidence is that when an ancient religion portrayed an animal in its rites or myths, the sole beneficiary has invariably been humans.

In this chapter, examples obtained from ancient Egyptian, Indian and Chinese religions demystify allegories and attributes given to animals, supporting the understanding of the real reason why they were used as a heavenly expression, despite never enjoying equal treatment as the humans who adored their symbolisms or their alleged relationship with the divine.

Egypt: iconography

In Ancient Egypt, the vast majority of gods were portrayed as having the head of an animal and the body of a human being. This is amply observed on temple walls, ornaments, religious statues and papyrus scriptures. A diversity of animals constituted the pantheon of the civilisation on the banks of the Nile River.

In the dynastic period between 3100 BCE to 2686 BCE, Anubis, god of death, mummification, embalming, life after death, cemeteries, tombs and the underworld in general, was depicted in the form of a complete animal – with the head and body of a jackal. After that period, the god began to be portrayed only with the head of the animal, hence acquiring a humanoid body.[1]

Predominantly, the Egyptians of the middle and upper classes would have a pet dog, as they believed that the presence of the animal, related to Anubis, could not only repel death, but also guarantee a satisfying and luxurious afterlife. Nevertheless, stray dogs or someone else's dogs were typically ignored or just seen as mere animals.

Although the correlation between animals and gods, especially in ancient pantheons, was based upon the personalities of the animals and the gods, as if one reflected the aspects of the other, in Ancient Egypt the subject had much more to do with a worldly view than properly with the divine.

In predynastic Egypt, when the dead were buried in shallow graves, the region's wild dogs would dig up the graves to eat the corpses. Thus, these animals were strongly associated with cemeteries. This explains the early correlation between Anubis and dogs and jackals.[1]

Yet another example demystifying the erroneous idea that animals in Ancient Egypt were considered sacred, relates to Ra – god of the sun, of order and the sky.

In the Fifth Dynasty, around the 25th and 24th century BCE, Ra had become one of the most important gods of the ancient Egyptian religion, identified mainly with the midday sun. Ra was believed to rule in all parts of the created world: heaven, earth and the underworld. The god was portrayed as having the body of a human and the head of a falcon.[1]

According to mythology, Ra received the personification of a falcon after creating the world and leaving it in darkness for 12 days.

During this time, Ra sailed through the underworld, illuminating the dead, destroying the enemies of creation and regenerating in a union with Osiris, the god of resurrection. When Ra reappeared at dawn on the eastern horizon, he took the form of a falcon, known as *Hor-akhty* or Horus of the Horizon, meaning "the falcon that flies high in the sky".

Statuettes of Ra (305–200 BCE), Bastet (305–250 BCE) and Anubis (332–30 BCE). Credit: Ra - Brooklyn Museum; Bastet - The Walters Art Museum; Anubis - Private collector.

Ra, the god of the kings, had such a symbolic appearance based on his creations, the sky and the earth. Thus falcons, with their allegorical ability to fly as high as the midday sun, privileged with panoramic eyesight of Ra's creations, were the perfect fit for illustrating the god.

Nut, goddess of the sky, the stars, the cosmos, astronomy and the universe, was represented by the image of a celestial cow.[1]

Contrary to what may be believed, Nut did not share characteristics with cows. Before countless misleading characteristics were attributed to her, Nut would be just a deity known as the agent of great causes.

According to mythology, Ra was tired of having to rule ungrateful humanity, thus, he asked Nut to take him to the highest heavens. Bewildered, Nut hesitated, as she did not know how to go about such a task. But the god Nun, father of Ra, obligated her, transforming the goddess into a celestial cow.

The symbolism of a cow was correlated to that of a "carrier", as cows would mostly serve as carriers and cart wagon pullers in Ancient Egypt. Additionally, receiving the denomination of a "celestial" goddess was intrinsically paralleled with the task Nut had performed, under the orders of Nun. Celestial cows therefore would suggest "the carrier to the highest heavens".

Nut was also depicted wearing a water pot as a headdress. The pot, which can be found in the hieroglyph of part of her name, suggested that it may have symbolised the uterus,[2] however, the amphora may also have represented the water carried by the cows, as well a bucket of milk.

Being represented as a celestial cow, Nut was subsequently linked to maternity. Nevertheless, the only reason why Nut was initially linked with the image of a cow was by virtue of being the carrier of Ra, not for portraying any maternal characteristics, which were, thereafter, artificially added to her qualities.

Hieroglyphs of the most notorious Egyptian gods.
Notice the parallel between the deities and the animals
used to symbolise them. Credit: Jim Loy

The goddess Bastet has been worshipped since the Second Dynasty (2890 BCE) in Lower Egypt. Originally, she was portrayed as a lioness, an attribute shared by other deities, such as Sekhmet.[1]

Eventually, Bastet and Sekhmet were characterised as two different aspects of the same goddess. Sekhmet, representing the powerful warrior and protective aspect, was hence given the image of a lioness, while Bastet, who had a more gentle and domesticated personality, started to be more related to domesticated cats.

The initial qualities of Bastet, however, were those of a warrior, linked to the sun and the battles, typical traits of a lioness, who is a diurnal animal, as well as an energetic hunter.

When Sekhmet was given the role of a lioness, it was natural for Bastet to keep her roots as a lioness, albeit a much more tame and delicate one. As a result, the cat was connoted to Bastet, who had her cult and worship maintained without major changes to her feline image.

Once she was represented as a cat, Bastet saw her personality adapted around the personality of cats. Thus, Bastet became the Egyptian goddess of the home, domesticity and women's secrets. Fertility has also become one of Bastet's attributes, as cats can procreate several times in one lifetime.

Mafdet was one of the first Egyptian deities to be portrayed as a cat. Her cult was prominent during the first dynasty of Egypt (3200–3000 BCE), where she was often depicted wearing the skin of a cheetah. She was venerated for protecting against the bite of snakes and scorpions. Later, those qualities would pass to Bastet.

One of the most fervent arguments for why worshippers venerated Bastet was due to her nature of keeping homes protected from evil spirits and disease. The ordinary animal provided the divine with their mundane features, as before being revered as a cat, Bastet had no connection with pests, diseases, or even home life, yet as domesticated cats keep pests away, especially mice and small snakes, these traits become one of the most renowned attributes of Bastet.

All in all, most of the gods of Ancient Egypt who were portrayed as animals were, in fact, gods who poorly shared their divine characteristics with their representations on earth. They were, thus, the victims of misinterpreted mythological correlations.

Nevertheless, it is crucial to highlight that regardless of being dressed, named and shaped by humans, those gods and goddesses were, and still are, real deities. Their existence was not invented by humans, but discovered. Neither were their divine qualities compromised by a constantly modified appearance. It is also accepted that several gods and goddesses obtained a different image and, consequently, different aspects as a result of a better understanding of their cult. That may suggest the possibility that the god's altered qualities were more appropriate to their nature, as opposed to their primitive, initial prospects.

A Cryptic Fraud

Undeniably, the Egyptians venerated hawks and falcons, since these were the supreme portraits of Ra. However, while worshippers of Ra wondered whether wild hawks and falcons flying high were Ra himself, on the earth, those same animals were often treated cruelly.

The Egyptians would mass-breed raptors to give them as votive offerings to the gods. Not only were falcons, hawks and kestrels kept in captivity for the sole purpose of being given as offerings, they were also force-fed to have a generous last meal before being mummified. The purpose of an excessive last meal was, assuredly, to appease the gods further. The birds would commonly choke to death. In contrast, other worshippers would prefer to have the animal gutted instead of force-feeding them a last meal, replacing their organs with other objects. It must be mentioned that the animals being gutted were not killed before undergoing such a process.[3, 4]

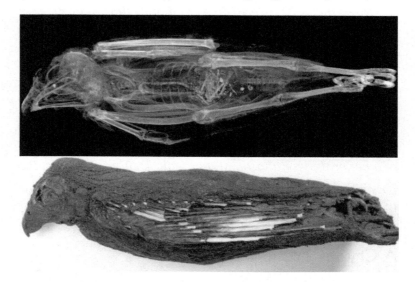

3D image of the mummified kestrel "SACHM 2575", showing the tail of a mouse extending through the bird's oesophagus, as well as parts of other animals in its stomach such as pieces of another mouse and other birds. The kestrel's meal was forcibly swallowed before the embalming. ©Stellenbosch University

When beloved pet cats died, they were embalmed, coffined and buried in cat cemeteries.[5] However, at the same time as they were regarded as the living incarnation of Bastet, other cats raised in captivity in order to be offered to the gods. Votive cats were, like falcons and other birds, given to the very goddesses they represented.

As offerings or as company for deceased pharaohs, they were mummified, which also included the occasional force-feeding to death, or rarely gutting, having their organs substituted by jewellery.

In view of the vast number of cat mummies found in Egypt, the cat cult was certainly important for the country's economy, as it required the breeding of cats and a trading network for the supply of food, oils and resins for embalming them.[6]

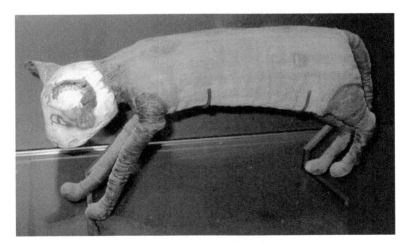

Mummified cat. Credit: Louvre

During the Hellenistic period between 323 and 30 BCE, the goddess Isis became associated with Bastet and cats, as indicated by an inscription at the Temple of Edfu: *"Isis is the soul of Bastet"*. In this period, cats were systematically bred to be killed and to be mummified as sacrifices to the gods.[7] Paradoxically, as described by the Greek historian Diodorus Siculus (90–30 BCE), killing a cat in Egypt was regarded as a serious crime. In the years between 60 and 56 BCE, outraged Egyptians even lynched a Roman soldier for killing a cat, despite Pharaoh Ptolemy XII Auletes' attempt to safeguard the man.[8]

During Egypt's first dynasty, circa 3218–3035 BCE, not only were animals sacrificed, but also humans. Human sacrifice was practised as part of the funerary rituals associated with all of the pharaohs of that period.

The sacrifices are clearly demonstrated by fee retainers being buried near each pharaoh's tomb as well as animals sacrificed for the burial.

The tomb of Djer, pharaoh of the First Dynasty, is identified with the burials of 338 individuals. The people and animals sacrificed, such as donkeys, were expected to assist the pharaoh in a luxurious afterlife.

A typical transgression among ancient cults in Egypt was the parallel created between honourable priests and misguided believers (including pharaohs), who ultimately perceived ritualistic customs based on 'religious situatedness' and radical devotion. In Egypt, numerous priests would not advise on human or animal sacrifice, but their suggestions were often disdained by many, including other priests.

Sacrifice in Ancient Egypt was prohibited by 380 CE, after a series of decrees and edicts issued by Roman emperors in the 4th and 5th centuries CE.[9]

Concerning the diet of the ancient Egyptians, Egyptologists believe that the rich would have extravagant suppers replete with meat, while the poor would have vegetables and a much more moderate amount of meat. The lower class would also raise animals to be used exclusively for food. Among the most consumed meats in Ancient Egypt were the meat of hippopotamus, gazelle, bull, duck and fish. Many priests would abstain from consuming steak.

Hippopotamuses and oxen/cows, who shared their images with, respectively, Taweret and Nut, were not spared for their appearance or similarities with the gods. Herds were fattened and slaughtered without ceremony or any liturgy.

The Egyptians did not worship animals as deities, but solely their image. Whether as sacrifices, food or forced labour, the animals of Ancient Egypt themselves were, without exception, not worshipped. Their connection with the gods was only their iconography, which served to facilitate people's understanding of the powers of each god.

India: synergy

In the Hindu religion, both in ancient and present times, animals are recurring figures in the worship of the divine. Some animals give shape to the gods; others are considered as the reincarnation of people.

Hinduism widely accepts the concept of metempsychosis, which is the theory that the spirit could regress to animal form as punishment.

The ideology may have arisen as an unconscious remembrance of their own exile to Earth, where spirits from different celestial orbs were temporarily banished from their planets, having to incarnate in less advanced species (humans) on Earth.

These concepts reappear throughout the history of Hinduism, which is often divided into "periods of development". The first period is the pre-Vedic era, which includes the Indus Valley civilisation and local prehistoric religions, ending around 1750 BCE. That period was followed in northern India by the Vedic period, which saw the introduction of the historical Vedic religion with the Indo-Aryan migrations, starting somewhere between 1900 BCE to 1400 BCE.[10]

Hinduism is the oldest major religion in the world that remains active. As Hinduism has survived the millennia, unlike what occurred in Ancient Egypt and ancient China, the primitive concepts that characterised its gods partially as animals date back to the beginning of Hinduism itself.

Several Hindu gods are portrayed as animals or have their characteristics: Ganesha has the head of an elephant; Lord Narasimha is half lion; Hayagriva has the head of a horse; Garuda has the head of a bird; Lord Varaha is a boar; Matsya is a fish; and Hanuman is a monkey.

In Hinduism, when such a god is portrayed as an animal, such allegorical correspondence serves to support the prompt interpretation of the god's most salient qualities. A similar scheme was used in Ancient Egypt and Mesopotamia.

In the example of the god Ganesha, it is observed that his portrayal as an elephant encouraged his cult to spread over the millennia, where only a fraction of the population could read. Hence the presence of allegorical images, which were crucial for the followers to understand the qualities of the gods.

The most well-known myth of Ganesha is the one taken from the Shiva Purana:[11] The Goddess Parvati had started preparing for a bath. As she did not want to be disturbed during her bath, and since Nandi was not at Kailash to stand guard at the door, Parvati used turmeric paste from her body and made the form of a boy, breathing life into him. Thereafter, the boy was instructed by Parvati to guard the door and to not let anyone in until she had finished her bath.

After Shiva had come out of his meditation, he wanted to go and see Parvati. However, he found himself being stopped by this peculiar child. Shiva tried to reason with the boy, saying that he was Parvati's husband, but the boy did not listen and was determined to not let Shiva enter until his mother Parvati finished her bath.

The boy's behaviour surprised Shiva, who, sensing that this was no ordinary boy, decided to fight him. The usually peaceful Shiva, now furious, severed the boy's head with his trident, thereby killing him instantly.

When Parvati learned what had occurred, she was so enraged and insulted that she decided to destroy the entire creation, and at her call, she summoned all of her ferocious multi-armed forms. The *Yoginis* arose from her body and threatened to destroy all.

Lord Brahma, the supreme Creator, naturally had issues with the intention of Parvati, thus pleading that she reconsider her drastic plan. She said she would, but only if two conditions were met. The first was that the boy be brought back to life. The second was that he be forever worshipped before all the other gods.

Shiva returned to his tender temperament and agreed to Parvati's conditions. He delivered his Shiva-dutas with orders to bring back the head of the first creature that was lying with its head facing North, so it could replace the lost head of the boy.

Thereafter, the Shiva-dutas soon returned with the head of a strong and powerful elephant, which Lord Brahma placed onto the boy's body. Breathing new life into him, he was named Gajanana and was given the status of being foremost among the gods, and leader of all the classes of beings.

Remover of obstacles, patron of arts and sciences, and also the "deva" of intellect and wisdom. As the god of beginnings, he is normally honoured at the beginning of Hindu rites and ceremonies. Ganesha is also invoked as a patron of learning, authors and bankers. Additionally, he is regarded as the god who brings financial prosperity. The mouse is usually Ganesha's "vehicle animal", which refers to wisdom, talent and intelligence. It also symbolises the detailed investigation of enigmatic subjects, as mice lead secret lives below ground. The mouse serves to show how wisdom is needed to overcome the erratic mind.

Ganesha portrays a generous figure. He is described as holding round sweets, which he is excessively fond of, and which represent prosperity. His trunk suggests flexibility and his large ears exemplify omniscience. Based on the portraits of Ganesha, it is noticed that his image is a theatrical illustration of his divine aspects.

Decoding Hindu gods is a complicated task, as their portraits typically exhibit a multitude of traces, myriad of details and several figurative messages in just one image.

The elephant is an animal of excellent memory and intelligence, thus the god received the head of such animal. It was also believed that mice frightened elephants, hence, Ganesha had a mouse as his vehicle, which signifies that Ganesha is courageous enough to defeat such dread.

Despite elephants being considered the incarnation of the Lord Ganesha, the animals often serve as symbolism for devout humans or as profitable assets for a few who exploit them for religious spectacles.

Thrissur Pooram Festival, Rajesh Kakkanatt. (Investigative documentaries have exposed the treatment of captive elephants in the region of Kerala, renowned for elephant worship and festivals.[12], [13]). Credit: Public domain

Hindus believe in ten avatars of Lord Vishnu, among a legion of gods and goddesses. One of these avatars of Vishnu is Rama, who was created to destroy Ravana, the ruling demon of Lanka.[14]

To help Rama, Lord Brahma ordered some gods and goddesses to take Vanaras (monkeys) avatars with them. Thus Indra, the god of war and time, was reincarnated as Bali. Surya, the sun god, was reincarnated as Sugriva. Vrihaspati, the preceptor of the gods, was reincarnated as Tara. And Pavana, the god of the wind, was reborn as Hanuman, the wisest, fastest and strongest of all monkeys.

The half-human, half-animal is a synergy noticeably present in Hinduism and in mythical figures from Ancient Egypt, Greece and numerous other cultures.

The image attributed to Hanuman is a mixture of the rhesus and the langur primates with human features. Hanuman has the most impressive and attractive aspects of each: the highly arched tail of the langur and the pink face with the most pronounced muzzle of the rhesus, as well as the posture of a human being. Characteristics of just one species were inadequate to portray a character as brave as Hanuman's.

Hanuman, the god of courage, has the physical characteristics of agile and athletic-looking monkeys. Appearing as an extremely skilled being provided the god with the quickness to fight and to engage in battles, which were likely to be won triumphantly by the energetic avatar. Combining a human with an animal, whose qualities give believers an improved understanding of a deity's personality, was thus needed to advance the cult of gods.

The qualities of three species were used to represent Hanuman's appearance. Nevertheless, the god emerged simple and primitive. This suggests that illustrators and sculptors played a major role in developing Hindu gods, and, perhaps, some of the many characteristics of each god may have merely been supposed after their portraits were made.

An Industrial Paradox

In Hinduism, animal sacrifice to the gods used to be commonplace, until the Buddha appeared and began to spread ideas of "non-violence", and that animal sacrifice contradicted divine love. Nevertheless, Hindus still kill animals of virtually all species for non-religious purposes.

Cows are worshipped as a result of the historical need of Indians to maintain a continuous source of food and labour. A cow that was killed meant that a valued agricultural labourer and source of milk would cease, thus, the idolatry of cows began (contrary to the idea that cow idolatry had started as a religious factor).

A religious meaning was later merged with the necessity of having what the cow could provide. It is still observed in modern days that cows will normally not be killed in India, however, they may still be seen pulling wagons, carrying loads and more notoriously, producing milk.

A pamphlet protests against the practice of cow slaughter. Chaurasi Devataon-wali Gai, or "The Cow with 84 deities" by Raja Ravi Varma. The man in the front of the cow with raised hands states, "please don't kill, the cow is the life source for everyone". Below the cow, a community of diverse backgrounds shares milk and dairy products. Public domain

Kamadhenu is considered the mother of all cows and a major symbol of prosperity. She is a miraculous "cow of plenty" who provides her owners with whatever they desire. All cows are venerated in Hinduism as the earthly embodiment of the Kamadhenu. As such, Kamadhenu is not worshipped independently as a goddess, and temples are not dedicated to her honour alone; rather, she is honoured by the veneration of cows in general throughout the observant Hindu population. Kamadhenu was therefore introduced to the scriptures for the need to symbolise cows as holy, as well as the embodiment of prosperity.

Although nanny-goats also provide labour and milk, cows produce considerably higher amounts of milk than caprine, for this reason, goats were seen as a source of meat instead.

Kali is especially venerated in the festival of Kali Puja in eastern India, celebrated when the new moon day of Ashwin month coincides with the festival of Diwali. During Kali Puja in Bengal, Orissa, and Assam, animal sacrifice is still practised, though it is rare outside of those areas. In the temples where the rituals take place, goats, chickens and, sometimes, male water buffaloes are mercilessly slayed.

Despite being the vehicle of Goddess Kali, goats are sacrificially offered, exhibiting yet again the recurring paradox of cults that symbolise the divine with animals while slaughtering them.[15] It is important to emphasise that the practice is dramatically becoming less common throughout India.

Many types of meat are used in Indian cuisine. Chicken, fish and mutton tend to be the most commonly consumed meats. Buffalo meat consumption is prevalent in some parts of the country, such as coastal areas as well as the north-east. The non-eating of cow's meat, however, is what makes most people conceptualise India as a predominantly vegetarian nation.

Anthropological surveys conducted in 2018 estimate that only 20% of Indians are actually vegetarians.[16] Due to cultural and political pressures, citizens report eating less meat, especially beef, while they report eating more vegetarian food.

Hindus are known to worship cows as goddesses since they correlate these animals to motherhood, kindness and tolerance. Therefore, killing a cow is strictly prohibited in Hinduism.

Cow's milk is also considered pure and is hence is used to bathe the deities' images. Even cow urine and excrement are also considered to be pure and are adopted in various rituals.

The god Shiva is also called by another name, *Gorakhnath*, which means God of Cows.

By contrast, buffaloes, close relatives of cows, are related to Yama, the Lord of Death, hence people do not invite them into their homes, as they do to cows. Hindus, therefore, do eat buffalo meat and drink their milk. The reason for such ambiguity as to why Hindus will eat buffaloes but not cows may be due to the late introduction of buffaloes in the Indian territory, which occurred millennia after cows were part of the Indian culture.

Although India may be stereotyped for the people's esteem for cows, it should be noted that the country is the largest producer and consumer of dairy in the world – both buffaloes' and cows', accounting for 18.5% of the world's production (2018)[17]. The production of dairy in India by species is as followed: indigenous buffalo 35%, cross-bred cows 26%, nondescript buffalo 14%, nondescript cows 10%, indigenous cows 10%, goat 4%, exotic cows (1%).[18]

India is also one of the largest beef exporters in the world, mostly buffalo meat.

More than 80% of Indians declare themselves as Hindus,[19] however, the allegories present in Hinduism with regard to the treatment of animals do not always affect the eating habits of the nation. According to the 2014 national census, 71 percent of Indians, who describe themselves as Hindus, are not vegetarian. According to official national research, vegetarianism is mostly observed among the higher classes.[20]

It is important to stress that the general population cannot be blamed for such a disparity between those who eat meat and those who abstain. However, it is relevant to emphasise that farmed animals are not treated with as much appreciation as is shown in paintings and mythology in general, and this statement includes cows and the local dairy industry.

Jainism

Jain dharma is one of the world's oldest continuously practised religions.

According to Jainism, the existence of "a bound and ever-changing soul" is a self-evident truth; an axiom that does not need to be proven. It maintains that there are numerous types of souls, but every one of them has three qualities: consciousness (the most important), bliss and vibrational energy. It further claims that "vibrations" draw karmic particles to the soul, thus creating bondages, but this also adds merit or demerit to the soul. Jain texts also state that souls exist as "clothed with material bodies", and entirely fill up the body.

I Jainism, karma, as in other Indian religions, connotes the universal cause and effect law. Karma is, thus, believed to obscure and obstruct the innate nature and striving of the soul, as well as its spiritual potential in the next rebirth.

One of the main religious premises of the Jain dharma is "non-violence", so as not to attract karma. Such principles have affected Jain culture in multiple ways, such as leading its adepts to a predominantly vegetarian lifestyle. Additionally to the diet, practically every Jain community in India has established hospitals to care for injured and abandoned animals. Many Jains commonly rescue animals from slaughterhouses.

Based on the categorisations of sentient beings and their perception of pain, the adepts of Jainism customarily will not even eat foods that may have harmed small insects.

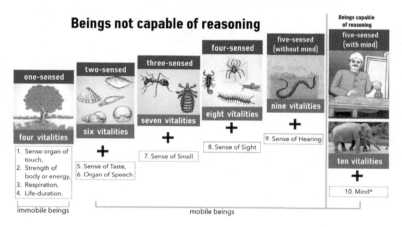

Jainist concept of Kinds of Saṃsari Jivas (Transmigrating Souls). Source: Jain, S.A., Reality, p. 62-63, 67

China: dynasty

In ancient China, the Shang dynasty ruled in the North China Plain, in the north-east of the country. It is believed that the Shang ruled approximately 13.5 people during their control, being the second dynasty and also an influential state recorded by traditional Chinese historiography. According to Chinese tradition, this dynasty began in 1556 BCE and ended in 1046 BCE.[21] The Shang were already powerful before out-ruling the

Xia dynasty (2070–1600 BCE). They were followed by the Zhou dynasty (1046-256 BCE).

The Shang dynasty is the earliest dynasty of traditional Chinese history firmly supported by archaeological evidence. Excavation at the ruins of Yin (near modern-day Anyang), which has been identified as the last Shang capital, uncovered 11 major royal tombs and the foundations of palaces and ritual sites, containing weapons of war and remains from both animal and human sacrifices. Thus, much of the information available about the Shang society has come to the surface as the findings of inscriptions made on bovine shoulder blades, or less commonly, on turtle shells.

More than 200,000 oracular bone fragments have been discovered in the Xiaotun region. The oracular bones reveal the most varied details about the Shang state. They wrote oracular inscriptions using 3,000 different graphemes and included a ten-day week and a 60-day cycle.

Shang emperors were buried in large cruciform tombs, the excavation of which required the work of hundreds of people. The corpses were placed in wooden coffins surrounded by funerary objects. On the ramps leading to the bottom of the tomb, human, dog and horse corpses were found. In that period, it was customary to sacrifice these animals in religious rituals to Shang Di (god).[22]

The Shang people worshipped a considerable number of gods, many of whom were living royalty. Others were spirits of nature, some of whom were possibly derived from popular myths and local cults.

Only with the Zhou dynasty would the idea of a main god arise. The evidence discovered in the tombs clearly shows that the Shang believed in life after death and that oracular requests may have been directed to deceased ancestors.[23]

The Shang court may have been frequented by shamans and it is possible that the emperor himself was a shaman. Should these views be legitimate, the essence of the Shang religion was assuredly different from the rational approach of the philosophical schools that would have become predominant during the Zhou period.

Chinese historians of later periods have become accustomed to the notion that one dynasty succeeded the other. However, it is known that the political situation in primitive China was much more complex. Numerous scholars[24] suggest that the Xia and the Shang were perhaps political entities that coexisted, as the Zhou were contemporaries of the Shang. Both dynasties had animal sacrifices as a norm in their religious rituals.

According to historians, the origin of the use of dogs as votive offerings developed from a primitive cult in honour of a dog-shaped vegetation god, whose worship later merged with that of Shang Di, the reigning divinity of the Shang pantheon, hence the systematic sacrifice of dogs at that time.

The excavations of Shang tombs around Anyang in 1928 revealed a large number of animal and human sacrifices. There was hardly one tomb or a consecrated building without the sacrifice of a dog. In Xiaotong, the bones of a total of 825 human victims, 15 horses, 10 oxen, 18 sheep and 35 dogs were unearthed. Dogs were usually buried wrapped in rushes and in lacquer coffins. Often, the dogs were just puppies. Generally, the dogs were buried alive, as they would serve as the eternal guardian for that human in the afterlife.[22] In a discovery in the ancient city of Zhengzhou, archaeologists found eight ditches containing the remains of 92 strung dogs, who were apparently buried alive. The fact that sacrifices were mostly of dogs and domestic horses demonstrates the importance of these two animals to ancient Chinese society in religious terms. This is reflected in an expression still used in modern times, "to serve like a dog or a horse".

Photograph of horse skeletons in the "Sacrificial Horse Pit", a burial site from the times of the State of Qi, believed to belong to the tomb of Duke Jing of Qi who reigned from 547 to 490 BC. Photo: Rolf Mueller

Pigs, sheep and goats were also sacrificed. However, this practice was only incorporated once sheep were introduced into China, shortly after the region began to establish trade routes with Indo-European regions.

Without special status or the right to live, it is an incontestable truth that sacrificed animals were not part of the religion, but mere votive elements, comparable to bowls of water and incense.

Shang oracle bones mention questions concerning the whereabouts of lost dogs. They also refer to the *ning* rite during which a dog was dismembered to placate the four winds or honour the four directions. This sacrifice was carried over into Zhou times. The Erya (ancient Chinese dictionary) records a custom to dismember a dog to "bring the four winds to a halt".

They also sacrificed dogs in rituals invented without the slightest doctrinal connection, as in the example of the *Nan* sacrifice to repel the plague: a dog was dismembered and its remains buried in front of the main gates of the capital. *Ba's* sacrifice, to intercept evil, demanded that the emperor, the "Son of Heaven", mounted on a jade chariot, crush a dog under the wheels of his vehicle. It was the duty of a specially appointed official to supply a mono-coloured, spotless dog for sacrifice. The rituals occasionally included the blood of dogs, which were used to swear pacts among nobles.

Only in the Han dynasty (206 BCE–220 CE) did clay dog figures replace the burial sacrifices.

Chinese Zodiac

One of the most prominent representations of animals in ancient China comes from the zodiac. The Chinese zodiac, which is a classification scheme based on the lunar calendar, assigns an animal and its qualities each year in a repeated 12-year cycle. The 12-year cycle is an approximation of Jupiter's 11.85-year orbital period.[24] Originating in China during the Han dynasty, the zodiac and its variations remain popular in many Asian countries, such as Japan, South Korea, Vietnam, Cambodia and Thailand.

The animals of the zodiac are the rat, ox, tiger, rabbit, dragon, snake, horse, sheep, monkey, rooster, dog and pig.

The order of the animals is explained with a folk tale about how animals were summoned to heaven by Emperor Jade, who ruled the skies over China. Legend has it that Emperor Jade ran a race and required all animals to participate. The top 12 could, hence, own a place on the calendar. Although the rat was small, it won first place, after being carried on the ox's back. The pig took the last place, since it stopped on the way to eat.

The 12 animals are divided into six pairs. In each pair, the two animals are complementary and cannot be separated based on their balancing attributes and characteristics.

While the rat is a symbol of wisdom, the ox is a symbol of diligence. While the tiger is a symbol of bravery and vigour, the rabbit symbolises prudence. While the dragon is a symbol of strength and inflexibility, the snake symbolises malleability and dexterity. While the horse is a symbol of persistence and indomitable will, the sheep is a symbol of peace and tranquillity. While the monkey is a symbol of versatility, the rooster is a symbol of constancy. While the dog is a symbol of honesty, the pig is considered amusing and fortuitous.

The range of animals depicted reflects the characters that can be compared to people or resemble traits of the human personality. From the adored dragon, mythical animal and traditional Chinese mascot, to the lamentably abhorred rat. From the dreadful snake to the harmless rabbit. From the pig, eaten throughout the history of China, to the domesticated dog.

Since the Han dynasty, the zodiac animals have served as a mere correlation tool. With the exception of the legendary dragon, practically all the animals depicted were slaughtered for food, which demonstrates that, despite being celebrated each year, those animals were just symbols to facilitate the correlation of personality traits, being granted no special status.

In many parts of ancient China, the killing of cattle and the consumption of cows was prohibited, as they were "valued" for their role in agriculture, similarly to what occurred in India. In modern days, such a custom is still followed by a modest number of Chinese families.

The eating of dog meat in China dates back thousands of years. Dog meat has been a common source of food in some areas from around 500 BCE and possibly even earlier.

It is also proposed by a team of geneticists of the Royal Institute of Technology in Stockholm, in a report written with geneticists of the Kunming Institute of Zoology in China, that a region south of the Yangtze River was the principal and probably sole region where wolves were domesticated by humans. The findings run counter to theories placing the cradle of the canine line in the Middle East.[25] However, it is suggested that the domestication of wolves in China served as a diet source, as opposed to companions and agricultural labourers in the Middle East, with archaeological findings dating back to 14,000 BCE.[26]

Additionally, in classical Chinese literature, dogs are generally described as treacherous, yet, paradoxically, they were used as an offering to the gods, as guards to those who died and as food.

In Ancient China, however, pigs, chickens and bulls were the animals most commonly consumed by the people.

Confucianism

Confucianism is one of China's greatest philosophical-religious, moral and political traditions. Developed over two millennia, it has also had an enormous influence in Japan, Korea and Vietnam.

A ritual system and social doctrine, which aimed to remedy China's spiritual decay, Confucianism was created at a time of profound corruption and serious political upheaval.

The notable importance attributed to Confucius in classical Chinese texts led the first Europeans who arrived in the region to think that Confucius was in fact its founder. However, such practices existed before Confucius. According to Chinese tradition, Confucius represents the greatest exponent of that philosophy and was, therefore, worthy of accreditation.

By emphasising family ties and social harmony between larger groups, rather than a soteriology that projects man's hopes for a transcendent future, Confucianism is defined as a humanistic doctrine.

According to Western scholars, Confucianism is a philosophical system that regards "the secular as sacred",[27] considering the common activities of human life and, especially, intra-human relations as manifestations of the sacred and expression of man's moral nature. Thus, man has a transcendent anchor in heaven: the god of the universe and his order.

Confucian liturgy regarding the worship of gods in public temples is ancient. After confronting competing schools of thought during the Warring States Period (475–221 BCE) and violently fighting under Emperor Qin Shihuangdi, Confucianism was decreed the "State philosophy" under Emperor Han Wudi (156-87 BCE), although not preventing the progress of other religions in the empire until the founding of the Republic of China in 1912.[28]

Concerning animals, it must be recognised that Confucius, the reluctant founding figure who has always been considered the "sage among the sages", left much to be desired on the subject. For him, animals were not part of humans and, therefore, did not deserve any philosophical mention.

In the Confucian tradition, god (or force), the heavens and the spirits should have all the attention and reverence, which plainly excluded animals. More than being ignored, they were sacrificed in offerings to those on the list to be venerated i.e. God, the heavens and the spirits.

Giving philosophic allowance to animals, or treating them dearly in Confucian regions, was seen as prioritising them instead of prioritising the heavens and, especially the family. According to that philosophy, if humans should live a life of spiritual development, the emotional mingling with animals should not occur, as an evolving human must expand this grace of evolution with the family and then with the rest of other humans.

Confucianism by no means prescribed the mistreatment of animals. On the contrary, it indicated benevolence and harmony towards all. Nevertheless, sacrifices were part of the Confucian way of life. Moreover, passages showing consideration to animals in the sayings of Confucius or Mencius, who has often been described as the "second sage", were almost non-existent, except when mentioning animal sacrifice; owning them as financial resources or labourers; and dog meat as being an edible meat.[29]

Taoism

Taoism is a philosophical religion of Chinese origin that emphasises living in harmony with *Tao* - "The Way".

Taoism, or Daoism, a term of Western coinage, designates the philosophical and mystical doctrines exhibited mainly in the works attributed to Laozi and Zhuangzi, composed between the fourth and third centuries BCE. The Taoist religion was institutionalised as such around the first century CE.

Taoism is primarily a cosmic religion, centred on the place and function of the human being, all creatures and all phenomena in the universe.[30]

Over time, several schools and interpretations on the religion were developed. Despite the ubiquitous distribution in China and the richness of the texts, Taoism is probably the least known among the major religions in the world.

Taoism differs from Confucianism in that it does not emphasise strict rituals and social order, but it is similar in the sense that it is a teaching on the various disciplines that aim to achieve "perfection" by becoming "one" with the unplanned rhythms of the universe, called "the way" or simply in Chinese "*dào*".

Taoist ethics vary depending on the particular school, but in general they tend to emphasise empirical spontaneity and the Three Treasures: compassion, simplicity and humility.

In ancient times, before the founding of the Taoist religion, food was sometimes established after a sacrifice of pigs or ducks to the spirits of the dead or to the gods. Thereafter, sacrifices were diminished to pieces of pork, chicken or fish, albeit still popular among Taoists. Those who had more financial conditions, that is, more animals, continued with the sacrifices.

In traditional Chinese communities, animal sacrifices are still proceeding. Archaeologists have traced this practice back to distant antiquity. Among the animals mentioned are dogs, chickens, turtles, oxen, and sheep. There is little textual evidence that Taoists protested these practices.[31]

Nevertheless, the Taoist celestial master Zhang Daoling (34–156 CE) rejected the idea of animal sacrifices to the gods. He destroyed temples that required animal sacrifice and had their priests removed. The rejection of sacrifices has continued to modern days, since it is forbidden to sacrifice animals in Taoist temples. The offerings, therefore, are based on fruit and incense. The burning of joss paper (ghost money) is also common, under the assumption that the offering consumed by fire would reappear in the spirit world, making them available to revered ancestors and deceased loved ones.

In Taoism, some sects linked to local religions used to practise offering slaughter. However, the cult emphatically preached the non-killing of animals. The sects which still use animals such as pigs, fish and oxen as offerings, are typically related to regional practices and folklore, diverging from true Taoism.

Buddhism

Buddhism encompasses a variety of traditions, beliefs and spiritual practices largely based on the original teachings and philosophies attributed to the Buddha, (563–482 BCE). The philosophy originated in ancient India as a *Sramana* tradition between the 6th and 4th centuries BCE, then spreading across Asia.

Based on the Indian principle of *ahimsa* (non-harming), the Buddha's ethics strongly condemn the harming of all sentient beings, including all animals. He thus condemned the animal sacrifice of the Brahmins as well as hunting and killing animals for food.[32]

Although early Buddhist texts depict the Buddha as allowing monastics to eat meat, this was a result of monks begging for their food and thus being supposed to accept whatever food was offered to them. This, however, was prudently tempered by the rule that meat had to be "three times clean", which meant that "they had not seen, had not heard and had no reason to suspect that the animal had been killed so that the meat could be given to them."[33]

The Buddha did state that gaining one's livelihood from the meat trade was unethical. Indeed, this rule was not a promotion of a specific diet, but a rule against the actual killing of animals.

There was also a famed schism that occurred in the Buddhist community when Devadatta (Buddhist monk, cousin and brother-in-law of the Buddha) attempted to make vegetarianism compulsory, but the Buddha disagreed, as he believed in the promotion of vegetarianism out of pure compassion for the animals.[33]

In the regions of Buddhist China, animals enjoyed freedom and the right to live, since the basis of Buddhism was the non-aggression to living beings, which prohibited the killing of animals, both for food and for rituals.

The Buddha promulgated many teachings encouraging non-aggression to animals, especially with regard to diet and offerings.

The Buddha's doctrine of non-aggression to animals was so tenacious that even the practice of sacrifices in Hindu India had also stopped after his appeals, and in modern times, Buddhists are usually vegetarians, abstaining from any food that causes animal suffering.

The Buddha is one of the most notorious religious references in terms of respect for animals. His teachings are still practised, hence, Buddhist temples and restaurants do not offer or collect food that is not vegetarian.

Although Shintoism is of Japanese origin, not of Chinese, it may often be inadequately perceived as a philosophy and doctrine indigenous to several regions in Northeast Asia, like China.

Shinto

Shinto, or Shintoism, is a religion that originated in Japan. As a polytheistic doctrine, it revolves around the kami: "gods" or "spirits" believed to inhabit all things.

In Shinto, many animals were used as a symbol of communication with the *kami*. The link between the *kami* and the natural world has led to Shinto being considered an animistic and pantheistic doctrine.

In modern-day Japan, the majority of the population follow Shintoism, which for its followers is not a religion, but a lifestyle.

Shinto tends to have a compassionate approach towards animals. Thus, animal sacrifices are not considered appropriate offerings, as the shedding of blood is seen as a polluting act that necessitates purification.[34] This notion of purity is present in many facets of Japanese culture, such as the focus it places on bathing. Purification is, for instance, regarded as important in preparation for the planting season, while performers of "*noh*" theatre undergo a purification rite before they carry out their performances. Among the things regarded as particular pollutants in Shinto are death, disease, witchcraft, the flaying alive of an animal, incest, bestiality, excrement, and blood associated with either menstruation or childbirth.[34, 35]

Various words, termed *imi-kotoba*, are also regarded as taboo, and people avoid speaking them when at a shrine; these include *shi* (death), *byo* (illness), and *shishi* (meat).[36]

Many *kami* are believed to have messengers, known as *kami no tsukai* or *tsuka washime*, and these are generally depicted as taking animal form.[35]

In Shinto, respect for life, including the life of animals, is one of the foundations of belief, hence, mediaeval Japan was practically vegetarian. The Buddhist vegetarian philosophy strengthened during the Kamakura period as it began to spread to the peasants. Those who were involved in the trade of slaughtering animals for food or leather came under discrimination. Those practising this trade were considered in opposition to the Buddhist philosophy of not taking anyone's life, while under the Shinto philosophy they were considered defiled. This discrimination intensified, and eventually led to the creation of a separate caste, the burakumin.[37]

National Japanese religions, such as Buddhism and Shinto, heavily promoted plant-based eating. Shinto also considers that eating the meat of animals is impure. But the rule extends only to the meat of land mammals, not marine animals.

Shinto preaches peace and purity, and, consequently, non-violence against living beings.

All in all, Confucianism emphasised human flourishing, while categorically ignoring the importance of animals, unless material affairs were to be discussed.

Taoism saw animals as emotional beings with souls. Worthy of human compassion, animals of numerous species experienced a certain degree of respect.

Buddhism introduced the importance of treating animals with thorough benevolence. Inspiring peaceful acts towards all creatures, the Buddha's philosophy promoted vegetarianism and other practices that aimed to deliver animals from cruel labour.

In Japan, Shintoism tends to consider animal mistreatment as an unclean act, seeing animal suffering as impure to the soul.

ANIMALS IN MYSTICISM

Totems

A *totem* is a spiritual being, sacred object or symbol that serves as an emblem of a group, such as a family, a clan, lineage or the entire shamanic tribe.1 Derived from the Algonquian word *odoodem,* meaning "his kinship group", a totem is generally understood as an animal spirit that an individual invokes, either for themselves or for the tribe. The invocation solicits, besides the spiritual presence of the animal in question, their special instincts and survival skills.

It was customary for Native American tribes to be composed of smaller groups or clans, united by descent and formed around a founding or ancestral member. This ancestor was often a symbolic animal spirit that became the clan's totem.[2]

Clan totems are often animals that inhabit the local area, having a unique relationship with the tribe and its history. The "supernatural powers" of the various totems guide each clan to accomplish their own duties and responsibilities within the tribe, according to the attributes of that animal.

Misleading mystical schools attribute the meaning of Western conceptualised archetypes to that of totems, assuming that a turtle would symbolise a slow aspect, or that the rabbit would connote multiplication, or that the wolf would be a plain hunter. The totems, however, abridge the notion of the surrounding animals with their own method of observation, which is unique as somewhat differing from such explanation from Asian or Eurocentric beliefs.

As an example of how Native American tribes may perceive a totem, a clan accompanied by the "turtle" endeavours to acquire the qualities of guardian of wisdom, legends and mysteries within their ceremonies and practices. Thus, the context secrecy subdues that of the sluggard.

Unlike Jungian archetypes, totems are seen by the summoner or the group as a totally positive and beneficial symbol, discarding any negative attributes that the animal may present in its personality or nature. It is not paradoxical that a clan would invoke the totem of a rabbit for battle. Even though the rabbit is presumed to be an easy prey (archetype), the totem centralises its meaning on the animal's cleverness and agility.

Upon summoning a totem, the individual or clan is bound to the morphogenetic fields of that species.[3, 4] This enables them to absorb the mixture of thought-forms created by such animals, allowing them to act in accordance with the instincts of that species.

*A Totem pole in Vancouver, Canada. Each animal
depicted on the poles represents the qualities that
the tribe perceives. Photo: Manish Tulaskar*

Although totems were part of the culture of the native peoples
of North America, the concept of invoking the presence of
an animal for protection has been growing in esoteric and
neopagan circles around the world.

Much more than a mere allusion to the essence of Native
American culture, spirits of animals and even disembodied
spirits of people who have morphed into the image of animals
may hear the call of who invokes them.

*Thousands of sinister humanoid spirits experience a sort of
metamorphosis upon finding themselves in the spiritual dimensions. Often, they involuntarily or voluntarily have their astral
bodies shaped into the form of animals, which may feature traits
such as a beak, horns, wings and paws. The metamorphosis
occurs according to the perception each spirit has of itself.*

*In the astral realms, the change of appearance is readily
executed by thoughts and how the individual feels they are. As*

the condensed matter is not required to give shape to an astral body, thought waves effortlessly fabricate what is believed.[3]

Here is an example of why morphism occurs: malicious and selfish politicians steal millions when incarnated, leaving many in poverty. Upon dying, their spirit may re-evaluate what was done with remorse. In this condition, the former politicians might develop a self-image of a vulture or rat, as guilt and the desire for self-punishment leads them to evaluate themselves as comparable to these animals.

In most cases, the individuals remain as humanoid spirits, albeit featuring animal peculiarities.

At the lower zones of the Earth's astral dimension, destructive spirits deliberately morph the appearance of monsters or ferocious animals, hence they can reign among suffering spirits and be respected through fear.

Thus, the intention of invoking animal spirits who are protectors may as well result in the presence of a metamorphosed spirit, instead of that of a real animal. Energetic vampirism is regularly the reason why these consciousnesses disguise themselves in such ways.

Additionally, individuals with a certain psychic ability, although bearers of corrupting egos, may have visions of animal guardians, not realising that it may actually be a case of humanoid-to-humanoid vampirism and not a real guardian animal spirit.

Demon Andras, illustrated in the book Infernal Dictionary by J. Collin de Plancy, 1863. Many demons from Goetia are depicted as being a morphism of animal and human. The similarity of these illustrations with morphed and vampire entities is remarkable. Credit: Public domain

Elementals

The elementals of nature are beings from the etheric kingdoms and the animal kingdom who dwell in certain layers of the astral dimension. Normally, elementals have aspects that resemble those of animals in nature. However, the vast majority of them have never been incarnated in the physical third dimension.

The primary function of the elementals is to maintain the balance between the subtle elements of the planet and support the transition of energies between the etheric dimensions and the physical dimension of the Earth.

In addition to supporting the transit of etheric fluids, elementals are also progressing in their own evolutionary stages. They are experiencing in the elements of nature the modality of physical life, albeit still at an etheric level.

Many of these etheric animals are called salamanders*, sylphs, gnomes and undines, representing the elements fire, air, earth and water, respectively. However, many other animals comprise this vast group, which is commonly found in unspoiled nature, such as beaches and seas, forests and woods, mountains and valleys, fields and deserts. Many live in intra-terrestrial realities or magmatic chambers on the planet.

*Legends have developed around the salamander over the centuries, with countless relating to fire. This connection likely originates from the tendency of salamanders to dwell inside rotting logs. When the log was placed into a fire, the salamander would attempt to escape, lending credence to the belief that salamanders were created from flames.[5]

Not all fiery elementals are referred to as salamanders, and most of them do not resemble salamanders or lizards of the physical third dimension.

Painting of a salamander unharmed in the fire,
1350. Credit: Koninklijke Bibliotheek

Elementals can be seen by humans via psychic ability, and the etheric fluids which sustain their life-form are often utilised by spiritualistic groups for a variety of energy healing treatments.

A poor discernment of what is considered "good" or "bad" is observed in the realm of elementals. For this reason, it is common to witness the deliberate use of their energy in low magic rituals that intend to harm others. It is hence recommended that such conjured fluids be used with discretion by witchcraft amateurs, as they can be severely destructive for the summoners themselves.

The spiritual element typically named "ether" is a subtle semi-physical fluid, known for giving life force to incarnated beings. The etheric body of animals and humans is nearly all composed of ether, in different frequencies and densities.

The term ether, also written as "aether", was adopted from ancient Greek philosophy and science into Victorian physics, and utilised by Madame Blavatsky to correspond to akasha, the fifth element of Hindu metaphysics.[6] English authors in the early 1900s also coined the terms "etheric body" and "etheric plane" from the teachings of Theosophy.

Despite the concept of angels being closely identified with Abrahamic religions, which refer to them as messengers of God,[7] angels can generally be considered all spiritually immaculate and benevolent beings who are intermediaries between the divine and the spiritual realms.

Because the Earth's elements are physical, their elementals live in the space between the physical and astral dimensions. However, 'ether' is a semi-physical element, as such, its elementals dwell in between the etheric and astral dimensions.

The elementals of ether will typically remain in the spiritual realms, without ever migrating to any primitive sort of life in the third dimension. That is, ether is not a physical element like earth, water, air and fire, therefore, ether does not prepare its elementals for an eventual migration to the kingdoms of the physical plane, i.e. aquatic, aerial, igneous, plant and animal. They may, however, incarnate in other dimensions other than the physical third dimension.

It is crucial to accentuate that elementals are embryonic forms of spirits who eventually migrate to other kingdoms. The migration occurs either to physical beings on Earth, if they pertain to earthly elements, or to other astral and spiritual realms, if they pertain to ether.

The migration of spiritual currents from one element to another develops gradually and by physical proximity. For instance, etheric waves of stones that accumulate forms of mosses or undergrowth on their surface, tend to enter the plant kingdom through the proximity between the two objects, which etherically mingle overtime. Subsequently, the waves that were once part of the stone, gradually adapt to life in the plant kingdom. The stone, however, must be in its terminal period of "life", which can be observed when it presents natural deterioration of its molecules. Such a process continues ceaselessly, hence, the final results take from hundreds to thousands of years to appear.

The etheric currents of rocks typically migrate to other more complex realms in their physical proximity. Moss is usually a one-cell per stem type of plant. Etherically, it is the primitive stage of etheric currents from an element (typically stone or aggregate of minerals) into the plant kingdom.

The energies of plants that had previous etheric existences as stones are, commonly, plants correlated to telluric frequencies, that is, plants that act on very materialistic affairs. Likewise, there are fire-related plants, which have conserved the fiery energies of ancestry volcanic rocks and minerals. Rue is an example of a fire-related plant; fern is related to water; and rosemary is akin to air.

The etheric currents of an entire mountain may migrate to the trees that cover it. The migration of waves and etheric currents may be imagined as thermal conduction. Thermal conduction is the diffusion of thermal energy between objects in contact. According to the second law of thermodynamics, energy (heat) will flow from the hot environment to the cold one in an attempt to equalise the temperature difference.[8]

Eventually, the etheric currents of plants and trees migrate to insects who live collectively. Subsequently, the ether currents of insects migrate to larger, more individualised insects and later to small reptiles and amphibians. The currents of ether customarily develop a more complex structure each time they reach a different realm.

The complexity of certain elements can be investigated based upon their interaction with the surrounding environment.

Mountains, rocks and an aggregate of minerals are normally under sunlight and rain, continuously interacting with the energies of light and water. However, they still inter-act very little with their surroundings, hence exhibiting the slowest migration to other realms.

Oceans, rivers and bodies of water interact with other elements directly: minerals infuse in water, light agitates it and gases merge with it. Water also models into different states: liquid, as water; solid, as ice; and gas, as vapour. It also circu-lates in the bodies of all living beings. The migration of water's etheric currents develops through thousands of years, albeit at a much faster rate than stones and aggregates of minerals do.

"Air" assembles a layer of gases that comprise the atmosphere of the Earth. Air is thus retained by the Earth's gravity, surrounding the planet and forming its planetary atmosphere.

In outer space, there is no air, but an absolute vacuum. However, outer space is not completely empty as it contains a low density of particles, predominantly plasma of hydrogen, helium, electromagnetic radiation, magnetic fields, neutrinos, dust and cosmic rays.[9] In these lines, despite being largely comprised of hydrogen and helium, outer space is still vacuum, which conditions gases as scattered matter. Therefore, only the elements assembled within the Earth's atmosphere are to be considered the basic elements of creation on this planet. Although the photons from the sun are conceived outside the Earth, they pass through the planet's atmosphere and become part of terrestrial existence.

Varyingly, plants and trees not only interact with the elements, they also combine, transport and transform them. A tree incorporates underground minerals and water while absorbing luminosity and gases from above ground. Therefore, they assist in the migration of telluric and aquatic ethers from their roots and aerial and igneous ethers from their leaves by propelling the basic elementary energies to experience more variation of states.

The interaction of a plant or tree with the environment is rather active, which designates their ethereal energy as the closest to that of the animal kingdom.

The migration of ethers from one realm to the other occurs during life, not solely at the time of "death". Elements, as well as plants and insects, do not have a structured soul; instead, they are endowed with etheric currents that sustain their lives. In this case, migration of ether (subtle energy) is less complex than the reincarnation of a spirit, hence it unfolds gradually during life.

It is crucial to accentuate that not every single animal, plant or elemental will necessarily follow that path, nonetheless, most less complex beings on Earth do so. It is, likewise categorically needed to emphasise that when currents of ether migrate from an element or object to another, other exterior currents occupy the spaces "left behind". Thus evolution evolves alongside the migration cycle of ethers from realm to realm endlessly.

Guardian Animals

The belief in animal spirit guides and animal guardians remain common to a number of animistic cultures and religions around the world. Unlike zoolatry, where animals are deities and numerous gods receive sacrifices,[10] animal guides and animal guardians are normally seen as friendly beings who appear to rescue or support an individual or group of individuals in their journeys.

In Celtic traditions, the behaviour of certain animals is seen as omens, and various deities are closely associated with local animals. The names of Artio, the bear goddess, and Epona, the equine goddess, were based on Celtic words for bear and horse, respectively.[11] In Ireland, Morrígan, the goddess of battle and fertility, was associated with crows, wolves and horses. In Scotland, Brighid was associated with snakes and cattle.

In the Celtic locales, animals were viewed as part of spirituality based on their physical characteristics, skills and behaviour. For example, stags, which shed and regrow antlers throughout their lives, suggested growth cycles; in Ireland, they were sacred and related to the goddess Flidais, while in Scotland they were guarded by Cailleach, known in modern folklore as the queen of the winter.

Beavers were seen to be skilful workers in wood.[12] Snakes were seen as emblematic guardians of long and eternal life, for being able to discard their old skins and renew themselves. Admiration and acknowledgement for an animal's essential nature led to the reverence of those qualities and abilities that humans did not or only partially possessed.

The animals seen as guardians of a group were typically envoys of the god to which those animals were related. At times, people thought that the animal was the gods themselves in animal form.

Celts would normally hunt after their gods' blessings and, ambiguously, they would sacrifice domestic animals in atonement for their theft of wild creatures from the landscape. Hunting itself may have been perceived as a symbolic, as well as practical activity in which the spilling of blood led not only to the death of the animal but also to the earth's nourishment and its replenishment.[13]

In European pagan folklore, "animals of power" and "animal spirits" are two concepts that have interchangeably evoked interpretations of a magical being. Nevertheless, an animal of power is usually physical, whereas the animal spirit unfolds as the spirit of an animal, intuition or the appearance of an animal-like spectre.

Unlike totems, which are invoked for their skills and a momentary stream of inspiration, the Celtic animals of power would appear unexpectedly when the individual genuinely needed them. The appearance of a somewhat rare animal was usually presumed by the Celts and Druids as an omen of power and messages from the gods.

The animal spirit, however, has certain extra-physical powers and abilities to teach, as well as knowledge to share. Thus, the appearance of an animal spirit would signal a moment for the Celts to connect with their purpose in life.

A pagan individual would not choose their animal spirit, instead, the animal spirit would choose them. Animal spirits would purely appear at the time when the individual is presumptively ready to accept their symbols and wisdom.

Each living being has been generated by a specific frequency of Source, hence, every animal has a different facet of the divine. As the black tourmaline correlates to rue, which correlates to snakes, the same divine essence is observed in all three species, regardless of which kingdom is assessed. In these lines, the animal spirit that shows itself portrays the symbolism of that divine essence in which it was created. This regards apparitions experienced in meditative and unconscious states, as well as in dreams.

Emphasis should be given on how to distinguish supernatural experiences from typical experiences in the physical world. Simply seeing an animal in the material world does not mean that messages are being given from a guardian or from the

*heavens whatsoever. Animals do exist on this planet to evolve
in their own worlds and not merely as a result of the existence
of humans.*

All in all, it is suggested that most manifestations of guardian animals occur in meditation visualisations and in dreams rather than in the sight of the material world.

Familiars

In European folklore and in beliefs that were specifically popular in the mediaeval period, "familiars" were considered supernatural entities that would assist witches in their magical practices. According to the records of the time, familiars would appear in numerous disguises, often as an animal, but they could also portray a humanoid figure.

Most legends mention familiars as small animals such as cats, mice, dogs, ferrets, birds, frogs, and rabbits. There were also cases of wasps and butterflies, in addition to pigs, sheep and horses. They were described as clearly defined, in three-dimensional shapes, in vivid colours and lively with movement and sound by those who claim to have come into contact with them, as opposed to later descriptions of ghosts with such smoky and undefined forms.[14]

Familiar spirits were believed to be kept in pots or baskets lined with sheep's wool and fed a variety of foods, including milk, bread, meat and blood.[15]

Familiars were considered malevolent creatures when serving witches, while seen as benevolent beings when they worked for ordinary people such as carpenters. However, ambiguity was present in both cases. The ones working for witches were often categorised and related to demons, while their counterpart familiars were commonly described and related to fairies.

The main purpose of the familiars was to serve the witch by providing them protection. In legends of familiars in France and Great Britain, these animals would appear in a predictable way or by means of incantation.

From the second part of the 20th century, modern witchcraft practitioners, including adherents of the neopagan religion Wicca, have used the concept of familiars, although the subject is still rarely remembered among these groups. For the association of such beings with ancient forms of magic, pets and wildlife are symbolically adopted as a means to manifest the ancestral tradition of having a "magical animal" nearby.

A late 16th-century English illustration of a witch feeding her familiars. Credit: Public domain

Archetypes

Animal archetypes relate to preconceived ideas regarding their symbolism.

The collective conscious is the set of shared beliefs, ideas and moral attitudes that operate as a unifying force within society. Ideas, in turn, are actually how individuals unconsciously interpret all that exists, and they are usually experienced as mental representational images of an object or an abstract concept. One view on the nature of ideas, also called innate ideas, is that they could not have arisen as a representation of an object of perception but rather were, in some sense, always present.

These are distinguished from adventitious ideas, which are images or concepts accompanied by the judgement that they are caused or occasioned by an external object.[16]

Another view holds that ideas are only discovered in the same way that the real world is discovered: from personal experiences. All eminent confusions regarding the way ideas arise are in part due to the use of the term "idea" to cover both the representation perceptions and the object of conceptual thought. This can be illustrated in terms of the scientific doctrines of innate ideas and "concrete ideas versus abstract ideas."[17]

In these manners, ideas can either be the perception of an object and abstract concepts as well as the theorising of an intention and suggestion. Therefore, archetypes are the primary ideas of all that exists in the collective consciousness.

The understanding of archetypes commonly epitomises the Jungian archetypes and Plato's theory of ideas.

In Plato's theory, the material world is not as real or as authentic compared to timeless, absolute, unchangeable ideas. The Greek philosopher defined "ideas" or "forms" as the non-physical essences of all that exists, of which objects and matter in the physical world are merely materialised imitations.

Carl Jung equivalently theorised that universal, archaic symbols and images that derive from the collective conscious are the psyche's counterpart of instinct. His theory of archetypes is described as a sort of innate nonspecific knowledge, acquired from the aggregate of human history, which prefigures and directs conscious behaviour. Just as the human body is a museum with regard to the long history of its genes, so is the psyche.

Jung also described archetypes as impressions of important or frequently recurring situations in the long human past. Detailing that, having our ancestors, and ourselves, experienced such idea several times, it settles in our unconscious mind, being able to emerge should a first contact with the archetype occur. Jung would conventionally correlate animal archetypes to representations of people's inner self, affirming that they would reflect hidden instincts, hence the use of creatures in numerous myths, which serve as lessons regarding human ego.

In an initial definition of the term, Carl Jung wrote:

"Archetypes are typical modes of apprehension and, wherever we find uniform and regularly recurring modes of apprehension, we are dealing with an archetype, regardless of whether its mythological character is recognised or not."[18]

He traces the term back to Philo, Irineu and Corpus Hermeticum, who associate archetypes with the division and the creation of the world; and also notes the close relationship with Platonic ideas.[19] These archetypes inhabit a world beyond the chronology of human life, developing on an evolutionary time scale.

The archetype of animals as symbolism and emblems observed in most world religions and folklores may also be described as the totality of experiences of people, which configures the interpretation of reality.

For example, when a thought about an apple arises, the subsequent ideas are of sweetness, the feminine, love, sex, mysticism. When a thought about gold arises, the ideas that follow are of wealth, luxury, prosperity, shine, royalty. Thoughts on the moon are followed by ideas of mystery, night, femininity, intuition, magic. Thoughts of New York bring the ideas of lights, greatness, conquest, power, the new.

Besides rendering a conscious meaning, archetypes act for the perfection of the idea or concept approached. In the case of an apple, its archetype invariably is of a luminous red, round, large, glossy and appetising fruit.

Some cultures believe that frogs represent prosperity. However, in the collective conscious of the world, frogs may also connote witchcraft and swamps. Therefore, it is crucial to perceive archetypes globally, not just locally.

Intelligence and technology are examples of abstract concepts. The thought of intelligence invariably brings with it the idea of the genius, wisdom, success and the prodigy.

Technology, in turn, summons the idea of futurism, cutting edge machinery and precision tools.

Ultimately, the archetype is an idealised and contemplative idea of an object or abstract concept.

A painting of Jesus Christ may be consciously interpreted as "divine" by a Christian and, contrarily, considered "vague" by an Agnostic. However, the collective conscious where the archetype of Jesus Christ is stationed applies the same effect to both the individuals: pacifism; compassion; suffering; and sanctification. This unconscious idea of Jesus Christ occurs as both the Christian and the Agnostic individuals interpret that character as an idealised idea or concept. Although the Agnostic individual may perceive Jesus as a fictional character, the archetype of such a figure does not depend on physical evidence as an agent for validation. Therefore, Jesus Christ is conceptualised equally by all.

To better understand how unconscious ideas overrun conscious ideas, the examples of well-known story characters of literature may support that claim – for instance, Snow White. Despite being a fictional character, the archetype of such a personality is universally established as that of an innocent, gentle, trusting and joyous young lady. Along these lines, human minds disregard the pieces of evidence on whether the object pertains to a physical or non-material idea. Thus, a film or fairy tale character is as real as historical human characters, like Napoleon Bonaparte or Mahatma Gandhi.

Archetypes are based on the strength of the collective conscious. In other words, an individual whose judgement on such a symbol differs from that of the collective conscious is still thoroughly influenced by the latter.

The presence and consequently the image of animals have a direct impact on the lives of humans, by triggering instant emotional reactions. The idea of an animal, in particular, connotes the essence they depict.

The assimilation of an animal archetype through their image diverges from what is known as "subliminal stimuli", which are any sensory stimuli below an individual's threshold for conscious perception.[20] Visual stimuli may be quickly flashed before an individual can process them, or flashed and then masked, thereby interrupting the processing. Subliminal stimuli and their affairs depend on the conscious mind directly, as they interact with what can be cognitively assimilated by the individual in a lifetime. Adversely, archetypes are pre-established ideas that do not depend on one's cognition. Therefore, archetypes are perceived by the unconscious minds, as opposed to what is perceived in subliminal stimuli by the subconscious mind.

Knowing the power of archetypes, trademarks, company logos, supermarket products and symbols on clothing and ornaments deliberately and openly influence people, albeit less discourteously than subliminal messages attempt to do.

Moreover, certain archetypes have groups of spirits associated to them. These entities typically ally themselves with a particular symbol and, therefore, connect their minds to such archetypes, including that of animals.

Archetypes are correlated to "dualism", which is a philosophy that assumes that the human being is composed of material and immaterial elements. Thus, the existence of archetypes is independent of the conscious mind, the thalamus or the prefrontal cortex, although it can considerably influence and be influenced by them. Archetypes are immaterial ideals, like mental holograms stationed in layers of dimensions related to the unconscious mind.

When archetypes are deliberately used in marketing, businesses and products, they maintain consumers and observers on a specific emotional stance, by delivering from the unconscious mind to the conscious mind all the sentimental meaning an archetype may hold. As a consequence, neurotransmitters, which are the chemical messengers produced by nerve cells, are discharged in the body.[21]

After the production of certain neurotransmitters and hormones, the feelings experienced by the individual are those related to what emotion the archetypes conduct. From the collective conscious to the conscious mind and finally materialising as feelings and behaviour. The effects of an archetype on the individual are, thus, the result of extra-physical and biologic processes that are inescapably complementary to one another.

By encountering an archetype, which is not only portrayed by images, but also as sound, taste, smell or general abstract concepts, neuron-association occurs in the brain. The neuron-association occurs when an idea intertwines with another, regardless of how compatible or similar they are. For example, an elegantly dressed woman who appears in an advertisement for a casino, donates those archetypes of seductive power and desire to the brand. As such, by neuron-association, observers may attribute such qualities to the casino, as the association between the woman and the brand is established in the brain, whereby ideas of seductive power and desire activate the brain's reward system.

The reward system is a group of neural structures responsible for motivation, associative learning and positive emotions, especially those that involve pleasure as a fundamental component, for example, joy, euphoria and ecstasy.[22] The reward system primarily motivates behaviour, which leads the individual to do something in order to receive that rewarding feeling, hence its name "reward system".

The gratifying stimuli influence individuals to behave in a manner that encourages them to have more pleasurable feelings, such as the ones from flavourful food, sex and video games. The same system proportionally influences the individual to refrain from less enjoyable sensations, such as those from sweeping the floor or other tiresome chores. In this competition, where the brain demands more behaviours that lead to the more pleasurable discharge of hormones, e.g. dopamine, mild addiction may develop. The repetition of behaviour for more of a certain sensation is interlaced with the lack of interest in tasks, people, objects and ideas that may not provide as much dopamine as the newly developed habit would. The repeated behaviour, therefore, awards the stimuli that generate the most dopamine, which annihilates competitor behaviours.

When the advertisement catches the individual's attention, the model in it is attractive enough that the individual pays less attention to their surrounding environment, and even to their principles concerning gambling.

Experimental psychologists make clear distinctions between "wanting" something and "liking" something, where dopamine appears to be important for "wanting", but not necessarily for "liking".[23]

When a dopamine rush activates the reward system, the individual's attention and focus are on the potential reward. In this case, the reward is not an interaction with the model in the ad, but the desire to experience more of what was just experienced when the ad was first seen. Therefore, the archetype of an elegantly dressed model defeats other casinos without such powerful associative marketing.

All in all, that casino uses the archetype of vanity and lust to propel a neuron association between the casino itself with potential consumers' brain areas that demand high amounts of dopamine, which may lure more clients.

The archetype of lust adopted by the exemplified casino would, albeit to a lesser degree, also affect homosexual men and heterosexual women, as archetypes are universal ideas of the collective conscious.

The archetypes of animals have an explicitly similar effect as the "person and brand" combination. However, the concepts carried by the various animals, also popular in advertising and logos, are abstract ideas, such as vitality, heightened skills and peace.

Popular brands that use animal archetypes as a logo.

The archetype of animals works as symbols, images and ideas, contrary to what may be interpreted as owning or seeing a real animal.

An archetype generally incorporates all the main qualities of the object, not just the ones assumed as "positive" aspects. The parrot, for instance, which can be considered eloquent, has an archetype constituted by connotations of gossip, imitation and limited movement; the elephant, bearer of incredible memory, exhibits traces of slowness; and the white dove, symbol of peace, may carry connotations of forced servitude, captivity and even cheap tricks.

Hens correlate to motherly love. However, as a result of the meat industry, their archetype is currently changing into unfortunate ideas of stress and apathy. Nevertheless, in the Age of Aquarius, due to commence approximately in 2150 CE, such an archetype will be entirely returned to its original aspect – that of love and motherhood.

Animal Symbolism In Alchemy

Animals were metaphors for alchemical aspects, elements and their stages. In these lines, eagles that fly high, represented the volatile ammonia; red lizards represented the crimson-coloured cinnabar; and wolves, most of whom were grey, represented silvery antimony. Serpents were related to the transmigration of the soul (for their skin-sloughing), hence they were the symbol supporting the alchemist who spiritually ascend.

Hermes Trismegistus, a syncretic combination of the Greek god Hermes and the Egyptian god Thoth, was the purported author of a widely diverse series of ancient and mediaeval texts that formed the basis of Hermeticism. The legendary figure is frequently depicted carrying a staff, known as the caduceus, with two coiled serpents around it. Metaphorically, the object was used to demonstrate his power and ability to transform his own shape. It has been argued that the staff or wand entwined by two snakes represented the god Hermes in the pre-anthropomorphic era.[24]

The Rod of Asclepius, on the other hand, is the symbol of the god of medicine in ancient Greek mythology. Asclepius' symbol is used in modern-day emergency medical services in multiple countries. The snake in the Rod of Asclepius would imply the healing processes, which is suggested by the natural renovation process of skin-sloughing.

However, a mistake made by many is to associate the Hermetic twin-snaked staff as the symbol of medicine, instead of the Rod of Asclepius.

The Asclepius Rod (symbol of medicine) and
Hermes' Caduceus (symbol of commerce)

Mythical creatures were also common symbols found in alchemy. Dragons represented mercury – as the metal used to be seen as an intriguing and peculiar material.

Commonly, the dragon would symbolise the four elements: the four legs symbolise earth, the scales symbolise water, the wings symbolise air, and the fiery breath evidently symbolises fire.

The three-headed dragon, however, was seen as the philosopher's stone and the elixir for eternal life, typically representing salt, sulphur and mercury, but occasionally the planets Earth, Jupiter and Mercury.

In most ancient cultures, dominating the dragon would mean dominating the material world and reaching spiritual ascension.

Several Egyptian, Greek and Babylonian protective deities are examples of bi-, tri- and tetra-morphism, which is an arrangement of different species in one symbolic unit. The Egyptian sphinx is also an example of allegorical morphism.

Following the examples of different elements in one item, the image of the Baphomet reappeared in occultism groups in Victorian England. Implicitly, Baphomet was the depiction of the four elements of nature. In its illustrations, opposites complement one another, besides the depiction of a spiritual flame which symbolises spiritual control over matter. Baphomet's goat legs symbolise earth; the scales in the abdomen signifies water; the wings represent air and the torch above its head represent fire. The duality between human and animal, as well as male and female, are also present. The face of a goat versus the torso of a human; the right arm and breast of a woman versus the left arm and breast of a man; one of the arms pointing above, a reference to the macro, which diffuses, versus the other arm pointing below, a reference to the micro, which concentrates.

Baphomet can be traced back to mediaeval times, being a deity whom numerous Knights Templar were accused of worshipping. Its name derived from an Old French corruption of the name "Mahomet" – meaning that the allegedly heretic Templars were worshipping Muhammed, the then anti-Christian character during the Crusades.[25]

*Left to right: Baphomet, by Eliphas Levi, 1856; A three-headed
monster, by Salomon Trismosin, 1582; and a dragon, by Friedrich
Justin Bertuch, 1806. Credit for the 'Flask' image: Wellcome Collection. Attribution 4.0 International (CC BY 4.0). Others: Public domain.*

PLANETARY TRANSFORMATION

The Status Quo

When the fundamental purpose of a work is to advocate the importance of spirits allocated in the animal kingdom, it is a moral and ethical duty to reiterate that a world of atonement can only progress to a world of regeneration when the noble and altruistic principles of equality between humans and animals are in harmony.

Status quo is a Latin phrase meaning "the existing state of affairs", particularly with regard to social or political issues. In the sociological sense, it generally applies to maintaining or changing existing social structures and values. Regarding animals, the status quo is assembled on the dolorous routine humans impose on other species. For such a doleful reason, the status quo must, as a prerequisite in the face of a new era, be reconstructed.

As souls, these maltreated beings involuntarily contribute to maintaining the planet's vibrational frequency at sunken levels.

Added to turning a blind eye to animal rights and their well-being, most humans arm themselves with excuses for the carnage these animals endure. The justification for the continuation of the slaughter fluctuates between the misunderstood diets of pre-homo sapiens; regional culture; and the occasional misinterpretation of religious scriptures.

The uncertainty about the cause for the deficit of peace in the world is typically accompanied by the financing of the butchery of sentient beings, which expresses a factual insult to any divine or spiritual law, regardless of religion.

Wars, heinous crimes, blackmail, slander and slavery of workers are unquestionably direct contributors to the paradigm of planet Earth remaining below salutary frequencies, which maintains it on a continuous pattern. The perpetuation of the existing social structure and values, which includes the slaughter of animals, is an injurious accommodation, which curtails the planet's ability to advance both morally and technologically.

Despite global hopes for harmony, peace and happiness, humans cruelly execute approximately 215 million land animals every single day,[1] (and that excludes the 4.9 billion fish and other aquatic animals captured daily).[2]

Each day, more land animals are killed for their meat than people died in wars, massacres, genocide and urban violence since the start of World War I. That is, from 1914 to 2021, all those estimated[3] 186 million human deaths are, still, less in number compared to the amount of land animals daily killed in current times.

The terrestrial psychosphere, which can be understood as the Earth's aura, and generated by thoughts and feelings, is severely affected by the number of animal deaths. Although countless doctrines claim that the Earth's psychosphere is continuously damaged by human to human crimes, resentment and mundane deviations, it often neglects the impact of such colossal figures from animal slaughter, which, as previously addressed, exceeds 5 billion deaths in less than 24 hours.

"Psychosphere" comprehends the spiritual environment of all living beings – especially those sentient beings, not just human beings. Thus, planet Earth can only progress to a reality of relative peace and spiritual regeneration once the world's leading cause of suffering ends.

The Expansion of the Universe

According to quantum theory, light is constituted of particles named photons,[4] the carriers of light itself, as well as other types of electromagnetic radiation e.g. radio waves. In the understanding of light, it is known that the electromagnetic spectrum is the frequency range of electromagnetic radiation and their respective wavelengths and luminous energy. On that wise, each colour in the spectrum has a different wavelength.

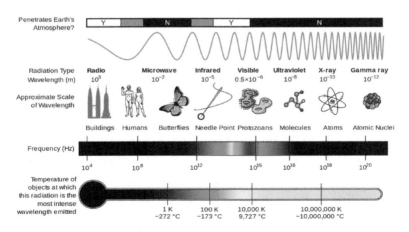

A diagram of the EM spectrum. Source: NASA

For example, the red light on the spectrum has a longer wavelength, while the blue light has a shorter wavelength. In these lines, when an object is in motion, a change in the wavelength can be observed, hence portraying a modified colour of the spectrum. Given an object travels towards the observer, its waves appear compressed (bluer) but if it is moving away from the observer, the waves will appear elongated (redder).

In 1912, astronomer Vesto Slipher discovered that light from remote galaxies was redshifted,[5] which was later interpreted as galaxies receding from the Earth. In 1922, Alexander Friedmann used Einstein field equations to provide theoretical evidence that the universe is expanding.[6] In 1927, Georges Lemaître independently reached a similar conclusion to Friedmann on a theoretical basis, also presenting the first observational evidence for a linear relationship between distance to galaxies and their recessional velocity.[7] Edwin Hubble's observations confirmed Lemaître's findings two years later. This phenomenon that examines the direction of celestial bodies based on the colours they depict is known as the Doppler effect.

Assuming such a cosmological principle, these findings would imply that all galaxies are moving away from one another.

The universe is expanding, therefore, the position of the planet Earth in the universe is never the same in space as time passes. This planet may seem to be in its exact position after an entire orbit around the sun, nevertheless, the sun itself is also moving and so is the Milky Way.

Based on numerous observational experiments and theoretical reasoning, the scientific consensus is that space itself is expanding, having initiated its expansion very rapidly, within the first fraction of a second after the *big bang*. This nature of expansion is known as "metric expansion". In mathematics and physics, a "metric" means a measure of distance, which implies that the sense of distance within the universe is itself changing.

Under the perspective of an expanding universe, the Earth will never relocate to the same point ever again (based on this cosmological evidence, which affirms that the universe is constantly expanding since the big bang).

The metric expansion also occurs at a multidimensional level, when the fields of consciousness expand their areas of operation to a higher dimension. The definitive correlation between the evolution of consciousness and the metric expansion of the universe is parallel and simultaneous, in what regards the moral and intellectual advancement of all species on Earth and elsewhere in the universe.

Astrological Ages

In addition to its diurnal (daily) rotation upon its axis and annual rotation around the Sun, the Earth incurs a precessional motion involving a slow periodic shift of the axis itself: approximately one degree every 72 years. This motion, mostly caused by the Moon's gravity, gives rise to the precession of the equinoxes, in which the Sun's position on the ecliptic at the time of the vernal equinox gradually changes with time, as it is measured against the background of fixed stars.

Simply put, this phenomenon induces what is known as the precession of the equinoxes. An equinox is usually counted as the time when the plane of the Earth's equator passes through the geometric centre of the solar disc. This occurs twice a year, around 20 March (spring) and 23 September (autumn).

In graphic terms, the Earth wobbles like a top, and from Earth's perspective, the constellations appear to move slightly from west to east at a rate of approximately one degree every 72 years. One degree is twice the diameter of the Sun or Moon as viewed from Earth.

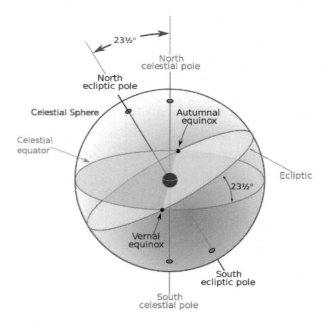

Diagram depicting the celestial sphere with eclip-
tic and equinoxes. Credit: Sanu N.

According to astrology, an astrological age is a period when remarkable changes are noticed in the civilisations of the Earth with respect to culture, society, habits and politics. Thus, it is postulated that the shift of paradigms observed in each era of the human civilisations spontaneously reflects the intonation of that astrological age, i.e. the constellation in which the world finds itself at that period.

An astrological age has usually been defined by the constellation or superimposed sidereal zodiac in which the Sun actually appears at the vernal equinox. Since each sign of the zodiac is composed of imaginary 30 degrees, so the twelve constellations fit into the celestial circumference, each astrological age might be thought to last approximately 2150–2160 years (72 years × 30 degrees). The Sun crosses the equator at the vernal equinox by one degree every 72 years; one whole constellation (on average) every 2160 years, and all 12 every 25,920* years.

With the earliest fossil evidence of Homo sapiens, archaeological findings comprehensively propose that the first modern humans appeared in Africa around 300,000–200,000 years ago.[8] Without methodical lucidity, the Upper Palaeolithic model theorises that modern human behaviour arose through abrupt cognitive and genetic changes in the continent, approximately 40,000–50,000 years ago.[9] Other models, however, focus on how modern human behaviour may have arisen through gradual

---

* The 25,920-year cycle, as well as the 2150–2160-year duration of each astrological age and the approximate change of precession of equinoxes moving one degree every 72 years are midpoint calculations. The variation of the beginning and the ending of ages is proportionately based on algebraic estimates, which were examined by several astronomers and cosmologists. The use of such dates in this work is built on the average of the dates surveyed, therefore, it does not reflect ultra-precise dates. Hence, the dates may vary slightly in the following paragraphs. The discrepancy, however, is negligible, considering it does not surpass ten years in each astrological age length.

steps, with the archaeological signatures of such behaviour appearing through demographic and subsistence-based changes approximately 70,000–100,000 years ago.[10, 11]

Despite attempts to leave Africa, which may have started around 250,000 years ago, the earliest evidence of modern humans of the 'out-of-Africa' migration dates back to 150,000 years ago.[12] Nevertheless, most of the early waves of migration out of the continent appear to have dissolved or retreated by around 100,000 years ago. The period of the first successful out-of-Africa migration occurred around 80,000 years ago.

Typical traits of modern human civilisations, such as agriculture, only commenced appearing in Eurasia approximately 12,000-10,000 years ago,[13] and human societies only completely transitioned to sedentary agriculture approximately 10,000 years ago in the Fertile Crescent,[14] a region that comprises modern-day Iraq, Syria, Lebanon, Israel, Palestine, Jordan, Egypt and portions of Turkey and Iran. The records of those first settlements unveil the development of agriculture, writing, villages and even the domestication of dogs, later contributing to the emergence of early settled civilisations from approximately 4500 BCE, initially appearing in Mesopotamia and starting along with the Bronze Age.[15]

A civilisation is any complex society characterised by urban development, social stratification, a form of government and a symbolic system of communication, such as writing.

Placed on archaeological findings and anthropological research, conjointly with the investigation of the history of modern humans, this unit attempts to construct an analogy between the history of the civilisations and the astrological ages, assessing their congruence. The aim is to trace a parallel of remarkable shifts in paradigm, e.g. culture, society and politics – and verify the affinity of such eras with the perspective of astrological theology, which claims astrological ages play a pivotal role in the unfolding of these time periods.

Nevertheless, the changing of astronomical eras, which is observed in every celestial orb, is not equal to the previous ones under the same constellations. The cosmological ages never repeat themselves exactly as they were before, as the planet resides, during each age, on a different locale of space-time.

Age of Leo – 10,750 BCE – 8600 BCE

The first settled civilisation in history were the Sumerians from 4500 BCE, nevertheless, it is pivotal to appraise the Age of Leo, for it shaped the world with an altered climate, vegetation and redefinition of coastal landscapes that made it possible for the first tribes to evolve into civilisations.

The Age of Leo, astrologically ruled by the sun, was the first age where the Earth had emerged from the last glacial period, which ended approximately 11,700 years ago.[16] Coincidingly, the planet, and most prominently the Levant region, were favoured by the sun's warmth and luminosity, which allowed the pioneering of the first agricultural way of living.[17]

The Age of Leo also covered the final period of the Palaeolithic Era, giving rise to cultures identified as Neolithic, first appearing in the 10th millennium BCE.[17] Those primitive, albeit structured cultures, drew their last breath during the Age of

Virgo – a methodical earthy period that prompted modern humanity to a future of farming and acculturation.

During the Age of Leo, numerous species of animals disappeared, while others flourished. The event may be presumed to have been responsible for the spiritual evolution and migration of spirits from one species into others. The occurrence equally affected the plant kingdom and that of humans, the climate being the pillar around which plant, animal and human communities revolve.

Age of Cancer – 8600 BCE – 6450 BCE

After the melting of the ice sheets that used to cover a substantial part of the northern hemisphere, the rise in sea levels occurred, thereby remoulding all lands across the globe.

That process caused sudden shifts in the configuration of coastlines, new irrigation systems, submersion and the merging of lands, salination of lakes, areas of freshwater and a general alteration in regional weather patterns on a temporary but also large scale.[18]

In astrological theology, Cancer is classified as a water sign, which associates the constellation to bodies of water, irrigation and, in particular, with emotions that relate to family identity and the home.

The Cancerian constellation, thus, enhanced the idea of the family unit, added to the concept of family members living in the same dwellings such as in huts, separated from the other individuals of the tribe. Thereby, the building of rudimentary houses started to take its first steps, marking the peak of the Neolithic Era.

During the Age of Cancer, the regions of Phoenicia, Assyria, Mesopotamia and Lower Egypt experienced the Earth's first proto-civilisations. These civilisations transitioned from nomadic to agricultural, with a more settled way of living which included the domestication of animals and farming.[14]

The Age of Cancer marks the first prominent transition that domesticated animals such as dogs and cats experienced, advancing from an exclusively instinctual nature to being affectionate and loyal to another species other than their own.

In spite of the domestication of dogs having started 6500 before that of cats, the relationship between humans and pets as cherished "family members" only occurred from the Age of Cancer onwards.

Age of Gemini – 6450 BCE to 4300 BCE

The written history of humanity was preceded by its prehistory, beginning in the Palaeolithic Era and followed by the Neolithic Era. During the Geminian era, ruled by the planet Mercury, language developed its structure as never occurred before.

Proto-civilisations started to revolve around barter, an exchange of food items done without the need for money or currency. This practice may have triggered the unfolding of a writing system, as individuals had to name and account for their rustic manner of producing and exchanging. During the 3rd millennium BCE, an intimate cultural symbiosis developed between the Sumerians and the Semitic-speaking Akkadians, which included widespread bilingualism.[19] Writing and grammar systems also flourished at that time.

The Sumerians (4500 BCE to 1900 BCE) were the first complex civilisation to appear on Earth. Propelled to civilisation by the migration of spirits from other planets, who possessed much more advanced knowledge than the spirits of the humans already inhabiting Earth, the Sumerians were the first humans to acquire modern rational behaviour.

Once incarnated amid the first civilisations, hence bringing the most developed essence to the human consciousness, those spirits aided in organising people in a structured society. Humanity would never be the same again, as the intelligent principle finally settled on Earth.[20]

The interchange between humans and domesticated animals also began during that period, making animals partially responsible for the formation of the first civilisations.

As the Age of Cancer emphasised emotional bonding, Gemini promoted exchange and communication, thus, generating an intellectually complex civilisation.

Age of Taurus – 4300 BCE to 2150 BCE

The Age of Taurus, which followed that of Gemini, was the apotheosis for the development of modern agriculture and the need for settlement, which marked the pivotal beginning of the first civilisations on Earth in Mesopotamia.

The Sumerians were the earliest known civilisation in the historical region of Lower Mesopotamia, emerging during the early Bronze Age. Living along the valleys of the Tigris and Euphrates, Sumerian farmers grew an abundance of grain and other crops, and the surplus enabled them to form urban settlements.[21] Thus, modern agriculture promoted settlement, which led individuals to desist from the nomadic venturing, typical of proto-civilisations. Thereafter, plantation and habitation flourished, as well as the accumulated produce, which was often used as commodities – a distinct Taurean method of ruling via economical means.

The Mesopotamian shekel, which was a unit of weight equivalent to the mass of approximately 160 grains of barley,[22] was first named in the region circa 3000 BCE. In that period, currency made of rare metals or pieces of adorned wood or stones also served to represent money.

Although the Sumerians were the first civilisation on Earth, other societies similarly blossomed in the Age of Taurus, notably in Ancient Egypt, Norte Chico (modern Peru), the Minoan civilisation (Greek islands), Ancient China, Mesoamerica and the Indus Valley.

The Indus Valley civilisation correspondingly emerged during the last quarter of the Age of Taurus, starting between 3300 BCE and 1900 BCE in what today is Pakistan and north-western India. The region was noted for its urban planning, baked brick houses, elaborate drainage and water supply. The Indus Valley was the most widespread civilisation in the world during that period of history.

The Age of Taurus also formulated religion and adoration. The history of religion refers to the written record of human religious feelings, thoughts and ideas. This period of written religious history begins with the invention of writing itself, approximately 3200 BCE.[23]

Apis, the ox deity, was the god of fertility. Linked to the king's power, the bull was the most important of the sacred animals in Ancient Egypt, from the Second Dynasty to the New Kingdom. According to Judaeo-Christian tradition, the golden calf also began to be worshipped during this age: when Moses ascended to Mount Sinai to receive God's ten commandments, the people of Israel, tired of waiting for Moses and God, forced Aaron to create an idol that they would worship instead.[24]

Egyptian statuette of Apis. Late Period, 664–343 BCE.
Credit: The Metropolitan Museum, New York

Regarding religious slaughter, some of the earliest archae-ological evidence suggests that the practice first started in Ancient Egypt.

The oldest Egyptian burial sites containing animal remains originate from the Badari culture of Upper Egypt, which flour-ished between 4400 and 4000 BCE.

Animal sacrifices for the deities and pagan gods endured until Egypt became a Roman province (30 BCE – 641 CE).

According to one of spiritism's most celebrated literature,[20] this was the period when most exiled humanoid spirits from other orbs began to populate the Earth, incarnating in human bodies.

The invention of writing replaced reliance on the spoken language with a more sophisticated method of naming and counting goods. Prehistoric proto-writing dates back to before 3000 BCE. The earliest texts come from the cities of Uruk and Jemdet Nasr, dating between 3500 BCE and 3000 BCE.[23]

As a structured civilisation, the Sumerians and their immediate neighbours promoted the advance of construction, design and detailed reporting for the first time. Lower Egypt also saw its influence burgeoning.

The Egyptian civilisation emerged during this ultra-materialistic period. Its pyramids were erected during the Age of Taurus and the techniques revolving around geometry also flourished. Like no other place, Egypt promulgated the concept of luxury, exuberant ornaments and the emphasis on guaranteeing a prosperous and secure life after death. Correlated to astrological theology, Taurus' concerns revolve around security, stability and preservation. Temples, jewellery and colossal tombs were reflections of such a Venusian period.

All in all, agriculture, a science closely related to Taurus, was accompanied by standardised writing and the arts, aesthetics and the accumulation of goods, making this an era that established control via economic power.

Age of Aries – 2150 BCE to 1 CE

In the Age of Aries, control by military power subdued the control by the economic power of Taurus. Civilisations founded on Taurus (earth) suffered a decline, while those of Aries (fire) gained space. What was built in Taurus was later conquered and raided in Aries, with barbarian invasions and conquest occurring in most of the northern hemisphere. Numerous civilisations also emerged in all corners of the planet during this period.

In the Age of Aries, human sacrifice became a notable part of worship in the Aztec culture. Additionally, the sacrifice of animals was a common practice, for which the Aztecs bred dogs, eagles, jaguars and deer.

Dogs were often sacrificed *en masse, especially to god Xototl.*

Similar to Anubis and his association with dogs digging up graves, Xototl, the Aztec god of fire and lightening, was commonly depicted as a dog-headed being.

The cult of the god Quetzalcoatl, for example, required the sacrifice of butterflies and hummingbirds.

The Aztec gods Xiuhtecuhtli and Huehueteotl were worshipped during the festival of Izcalli. For ten days preceding the festival, various animals would be captured by the people, to be thrown into the fire on the night of celebration.[25]

The Greek civilisation was also rising in the Arian Age, beginning in Mycenae, which was the last phase of the Bronze Age in Ancient Greece, spanning the period from approximately 1600–1100 BCE. The Mycenaean civilisation represents the first advanced and distinctively Greek civilisation in mainland Greece, with its palatial states, urban organisation, works of art and writing system.[26] This civilisation evolved into the Greek Dark Ages and subsequently to Archaic Greece and finally to Classical Greece.[27] All of these periods occurred during the Age of Aries.

The Roman Kingdom (753 BCE – 509 BCE) gave rise to the combative Roman Republic (509 BCE – 27 BCE), expanding its hegemony over the entire Mediterranean sea.

The image of the wise priest or elderly figure as a leader receded with the awakening of the younger, stubborn and masculine archetype. Typical Arian characteristics were also evident with systematic law-making, standardised hierarchies, division of classes, castes and corrections for "order".

As an example of how aggressive punishment became normal, Hammurabi, the sixth king of the First Babylonian Dynasty (1792 BCE to 1750 BCE) issued the Code of Hammurabi, which he claimed to have received from Shamash, the Babylonian god of justice. Unlike earlier Sumerian law codes, such as the Code of Ur-Nammu, which had focused on compensating the victim of the crime, the Law of Hammurabi was one of the first law codes to place greater emphasis on the physical punishment of the perpetrator.

The Code of Hammurabi and the Law of Moses in the Old Testament share numerous similarities. Despite being written between 1200 BCE and 165 BCE,[28] during the Age of Aries, the stories recorded in the Old Testament usually depict the previous period in history,[29] i.e. the Age of Taurus. It is also observed that, despite telling stories of the Age of Taurus, the Old Testament is intrinsically vindictive, a common trait of fiery Aries when in its negative aspect.

The implacable personality of God may be observed in several narratives of the Old Testament, such as when Adam and Eve are expelled from Eden to a hostile land as a punishment. This allegory may be theorised as the exile of spirits from Capella (the brightest star in the Auriga constellation) to planet Earth.

In their native world, the Capellians were jubilant beings. However, some were somewhat hostile towards one another, therefore compromising harmony among the benevolent spirits. Thereupon, a compulsory spiritual exodus occurred, so Earth could benefit from the intellectual advancement of such newcomer spirits, at the same time that those same spirits would polish their appreciation and empathy in Earth's torrid new times.[20]

An astrological age may also be lightly influenced by its opposite zodiac sign. Referring to the precession of the Equinoxes, as the Sun crosses one constellation in the northern hemisphere's Vernal Equinox (on 20 March), it will cross the opposite sign in the Autumn Equinox in the southern hemisphere. As the opposite zodiac sign to Aries is Libra, duality was also prominently observed in that period. As a consequence, the Hammurabi Code, as well as the laws established across the civilisations of the Middle East, Egypt's New Kingdom and Greece also possessed the first codes to establish the presumption of innocence.

Highlighting the creation of amnesty and balance of Libra, in 1259 BCE the first peace treaty was created between Egypt and Hatti (Anatolia and the Kingdom of Hattusa, modern-day Turkey). Archaeologists found the treaty's original inscriptions in both Egyptian and Hittite versions. The Hittite version is, exceptionally, told in the Bible as the Treaty of alliance between Hattusili, King of the Hittites and the Pharaoh Ramesses II of Egypt.[30]

During this age, men mastered metal more than ever before, leading to this era ruled by Mars being called the Iron Age[31].

The smelting of iron weaponry replaced that of bronze casting. Iron swords, crafted in Anatolia for the first time, replaced the heavy and warping swords of the Taurean Bronze Age, enhancing the region's military pre-eminence.

In China, numerous dynasties ruled during the Age of Aries, including, in consecutive order, the Xia, Shang, Zhou and Qin Dynasty, all known for their weaponry inventions and protective wall-building.

In India, the Vedas, the oldest body of religious scriptures, have been transmitted orally since the second millennium BCE with the help of elaborate mnemonic techniques.[32] The written form of these religious texts only appeared between 1500 and 1200 BCE.

The Age of Taurus was a period of polytheism, however, in the Age of Aries a possible inclination towards monotheism also emerged during the Vedic period in Iron Age South Asia. The Rigveda exhibits notions of monism of the Brahman, particularly in the comparatively late tenth book, which is dated to the early Iron Age, e.g. in the Nasadiya sukta.[33]

Since the sixth century BCE, Zoroastrians have believed in the supremacy of one God above all: Ahura Mazda, as the "Maker of All" and the first being before all others.[34]

Between 1353–1336 BCE, ceremonial monotheism took its first steps in Egypt with Akhenaten's Great Hymn to the Aten.[35] However, subsequent rulers returned to the traditional polytheistic religion and the pharaohs associated with atheism were erased from Egyptian records.

The statuaries of bulls (Taurus) were gradually being replaced by those of the ram (Aries). Interestingly, in a narrative in the Old Testament, Moses destroyed the golden calf when he led the Israelites out of Egypt.[36]

In the Old Testament, human sacrifices were rare, but did exist. For instance, in the book of 2 Kings 3:27, the King of Moab gives his firstborn son and heir as a whole burnt offering. In the book of Genesis 22 God tests Abraham by asking him to present his son Isaac as a sacrifice on mount Moriah. Abraham obeys this command without arguing, binding his son on an altar. The story ends with an angel stopping Abraham at the last moment, providing a ram to be sacrificed instead. This may symbolise the Age of Aries (the ram), but numerous biblical scholars[37] have suggested this story's origin was a remembrance of an era when human sacrifice was abolished in favour of animal sacrifice.

Adoration of the Mystic Lamb, 1432. The lamb has a wound on its breast from which blood gushes into a golden chalice, yet it shows no outward expression of pain, a reference to Christ's sacrifice. Credit: Hubert and Jan van Eyck

It is widely agreed that, as the coming of the Age of Pisces, the book of Hebrews 10:10 (New Testament) declared that neither human nor animal sacrifice was needed thereafter, as Jesus had been the final sacrifice. It is also believed that the place of Isaac's binding, Moriah, later became Jerusalem, the city of Jesus' future crucifixion.

Age of Pisces – 1 CE to 2150 CE

The Age of Pisces is the embodiment of monotheism, world religions and control via belief. Sects flourished like never before and sacred symbolism escalated in all civilisations.

According to astrological theology, Pisces is traditionally ruled by Jupiter, a planet commonly associated with the principles of growth and expansion. Contemporaneously, Pisces is ruled by Neptune, a planet associated with illusion and deception (when in its negative aspect). Thus, the two planets assumably propagate delusional religion during this era. Moreover, the expansion and faith of Jupiter multiplied populations and religions, whereas delusional and escapist Neptune moulded them.

After the astronomical discovery of Neptune, in 1846, the planet was attributed to Pisces, as it had been named after the Roman god, ruler of the oceans. The name Neptune was given by its discoverer, Urbain Le Verrier, as the planet presents a deep ocean blue colour, which prompted the astronomer to connect it to the oceans. The 14 moons of Neptune were also named after minor sea deities of Roman and Greek mythology.

The central symbol of the Age of Pisces is naturally the fish, which frequently symbolised Jesus Christ in primitive

Christianity (different to what may be assumed, the cross only became Christianity's main symbol in the fourth century CE).

Licinia Amias' funerary marble stele.Early 3rd century CE. Vatican Necropolis, Rome. Photo: Marie-Lan Nguyen

Jesus, who is the basis of the New Testament, carries several traits of Pisces, such as serenity over anger, which noticeably distanced him from the vengeful god and his rules common in the Old Testament (written during the Age of Aries).

As the most prominent character of the Age of Pisces, Jesus was surrounded by Piscean symbolism across various narratives, e.g. walking on water – a Piscean element; changing water into wine – a beverage associated with Neptune; washing feet – the body part associated with Pisces; the multiplication of fish; and for the 12 apostles, who were nearly all known as fishermen.

"AD" signifies "Anno Domini", which translates to "in the year of our Lord", meaning the birth of Jesus. Therefore, all dates

which are classified as BCE (Before Common Era, or alternatively, BC for "before Christ and BCE for "Before Christ Era") occurred before the birth of Jesus. CE, thus meaning "Common Era", or alternatively, Christ Era) refers to the dates after the birth of Jesus.

Numerous empires have changed the calendars in order to integrate their gods' names, holidays and celebrations. The Assyrian, the Babylonian, the Persian, the Greek, the Roman, the Julian and the Gregorian calendars all start their year in different seasons. Therefore, with each change, there is potentially an approximate six-month variance from empire to empire, affecting several years of the count when Jesus was born.[38] In this presumption of calendar alteration, Jesus is believed to have been born in 7 BCE. Consequently, precise dates paralleling the beginning of the Piscean Age and his birth may vary, however, the discrepancy is negligible, considering it does not surpass ten years.

A passage in the Gospel of Matthew 2:1, which is also a historical evidence, stated that *"Jesus was born in Bethlehem of Judea in the days of King Herod"*. Such a passage can indicate the exact date of his birth, which supposedly marks the beginning of the Age of Pisces. As a historical event, King Herod died in Jericho in 4 BCE.[39] Thus, Jesus would have to have been born before Herod's death, since the king would play a significant role in Christ's narratives throughout his life.

The nativity accounts in the New Testament gospels of Matthew and Luke do not mention a date or time of year for the birth of Jesus, nevertheless, it is believed that his birth was not on the 25th of December, although officially placed on this date to connect pagan celebrations with the birth of Christ, entrancingly replacing Roman paganism with Christianity.

The *Saturnalia*, a Roman feast for Saturn, was associated with the winter solstice.[40] Saturnalia was held on the 17th of December of the Julian calendar and later expanded with festivities around the 23rd of December.

The Roman festival of *Dies Natalis Solis Invicti* has also been suggested as the origin for the Christmas date, since it was celebrated on the 25th of December and was associated with prominent Roman emperors. Natalis Solis was a feast day observed as the point when the cold winter is defeated and the sun is reborn.[41]

Alternately, the 25th of December may have been selected due to its proximity to the winter solstice because of its symbolic theological significance. After the solstice, the days begin to lengthen with longer hours of sunlight, which primitive Christians saw as representing the light of Christ entering the world. This symbolism applies equally to the celebration of the Nativity of Saint John the Baptist on the 25th of June, near the summer solstice. Based on an observation about Jesus in the Gospel According to John 3:30, *"He must increase; I must decrease"*, it is believed that he refers to the equinoxes.

Intriguingly, in 7 BCE, Jupiter and Saturn were in astronomical conjunction,[42] forming what appeared to be a much brighter star in the sky, which may be correlated to the Bethlehem Star – the guiding sign for the wise men to find newborn Jesus.

The wise men were referred to in Greek as *'magi'*, which is the root for the words 'magic' and 'magician', present in most European languages. Along these lines, it is assertively assumed that the wise men were, in fact, astrologers. It is vital to highlight that the Greek word *magi* may have been mistranslated, considering that the New Testament was originally written in Koine Greek, different from the Old Testament, which had been written in Hebrew and Aramaic.

Supporting the claims of the exact year Jesus was born, when studying the great conjunction of 1603, Johannes Kepler thought that the Star of Bethlehem might have been the result of a great conjunction. He then calculated that a triple conjunction of Jupiter and Saturn indeed occurred in 7 BCE, confirming the idea.[42]

As for the pious qualities of Pisces, the vindictive fire of Aries was renewed with the waters of baptism, which replaced the sacrifices and cremation of rams, common among jews and other religious groups.

Mysticism unfolded from practically every ancient religion. Hermeticism was one of the most celebrated esoteric philosophies of the Piscean Age, as it refers to the secrets of creation and magic.

Alchemy is indubitably another natural philosophy and proto-scientific tradition that attempted to purify, mature and perfect certain materials, including the soul. Several doctrines used alchemy to theorise spiritual ascension, transforming one's consciousness into its more admirable form.

Gnosticism, which is a collection of religious ideas and systems originating in the first century CE amid early Christians and Jewish sects, emphasised personal spiritual knowledge (gnosis) over the orthodox teachings, traditions and authority of the church.

Ritualistic magic and occult sciences, where individuals do not depend on religious norms or tradition, became prominent in countless cultures.

Pythagoras's Philosophy of Ethics, Aristotle's Metaphysics and Psychology and Plato's Spiritualist Paradoxes: themes emerged at the end of the Aries-Libra era flourished and bore fruits in the Age of Pisces. Such thoughts became the foundation of Western philosophy.

The concept that heaven is elsewhere or impossible to be reached shaped the development of several religions.

Shame and anger, connected to the shadowy side of Aries, was replaced by the guilt and pessimism of Pisces. Among the interminable guilt and egoistic aberrations of that era, self-flagellation, tithes, indulgences for admission to heaven and the 'holy inquisition' were strongly advocated by religious priests, temples, emperors and kings. Thus, the religion disseminated in this era is characterised by dogmatic rules, where what is taught is imposed by fear and guilt.

One of the negative aspects of Pisces regards holy wars and conflicts in the name of god. Mass sacrifice for the Divine is also an extrusive trait of the Piscean negativity. The practice of human sacrifice in pre-Columbian cultures, in particular Mesoamerican and Andean cultures, is well documented both in the archaeological records and in written sources about the Olmecs,[43] Mayans,[44] Teotihuacan,[45] and most infamously, the Aztecs, who would even eat their children in certain rituals.[46]

The first centuries of the Roman Empire (27 BCE – 476 CE) were marked by a period of unprecedented stability and prosperity known as the *Pax Romana*, "Roman Peace". Despite the incidentally more bellicose Roman Republic, the Roman Empire was generally less forgiving, thus, emblematically Piscean punishment became common. Long-term prison replaced several acts of public torture and brutal deaths that quenched the thirst of curious mobs during the previous Age.

The Romans succeeded in maintaining their territories via the religion of Pisces while maintaining its politics via the traits of Virgo (Pisces' opposite sign). The *Pax Deorum* was a principle of incorporating or combining local divinities to the gods of the Roman pantheon, making religion consistently in agreement with their politics. Locals who had their territory invaded would benefit from having their deities recognised, and the Roman gods would secure unceasing worship.

Christians rose to positions of power in the fourth century following the Edict of Milan of 313, as the Latin of the Romans evolved into the Romance languages of the mediaeval and modern world.

Subsequently, the collapse of centralised authority in Europe gave rise to the Middle Ages (5th to 15th century CE), a period shaped by religious extremism, mass migration, monarchies, superstitions and astronomy.

The great navigations are also qualities of this age, as Pisces rules the deep and vast waters into the unknown.

Subjection and suffering are among the negative qualities of Pisces. Following these lines of reasoning, it is observed that slavery *en masse* was consolidated in all inhabited continents.

Although animal husbandry had started in previous ages, added to religious animal sacrifice, which can be verified amongst most ancient civilisations, the Age of Pisces depicts a magnitude of exploitation never before witnessed in Earth's history. Until modern times, the slaughter of animals generally occurred in a haphazard and unregulated manner in diverse places. The slaughter was then in the open air or undercover, such as at wet markets.

Increased concerns about animal slaughtering in the eighteenth century resulted in "public slaughterhouse" reforms, which marked the beginning of the concentration of animal slaughter and its movement away from the gaze of the public. Thus, slaughterhouses became industrialised, as exemplified by the development of the notorious Union Stockyard in Chicago during the late nineteenth century.[47] In previous eras, animals used to be domesticated to provide meat. This meant constant contact between animals and humans was common, which may indicate a cold trait in the latter.

With the advent of abattoirs in the post-domestic era, where people are physically and psychologically separated from the animals that they consume,[47] systematic carnage escalated to mass production, combined with consumerism, a social and economic order that encourages the acquisition of goods and services in ever-increasing amounts. One negative aspect of Pisces is that it is prone to addiction, secrecy and confinement, which may implicitly be associated to the existence of modern-day slaughterhouses.

Number of Land Animals Killed for Meat in 2013

Animals	Number Killed
Chickens	61,171,973,510
Ducks	2,887,594,480
Pigs	1,451,856,889
Rabbits	1,171,578,000
Geese	687,147,000
Turkeys	618,086,890
Sheep	536,742,256
Goats	438,320,370
Cattle	298,799,160
Rodents	70,371,000
Pigeons and other birds	59,656,000
Buffalo	25,798,819
Horses	4,863,367
Donkeys and mules	3,478,300
Camels and other camelids	3,298,266

Food and Agriculture Organization of the United Nations (FAO). The data does not include aquatic animals, eggs, experimented animals, skins or discarded chicks. Source: FAO

Pisces governs hidden and unpopular subjects, such as marginalised groups, slaughterhouses and fantasies. The main characteristic of Pisces is self-seclusion in its own parallel world. These traits lead to an era of an anaesthetised society, for which covers up unconscious guilt.

As denial is a blatant Piscean trait, most humans deny the origins of meat and are reluctant to discuss such topics.

Pisces governs illusion and escapism, all of which are vastly present in religious sects, but also present in the forms of alluring arts, as seen during the Renaissance. Additionally, Pisces granted the affluence of theatre, music and novels, besides the use of narcotics as a method of escapism or access to different states of consciousness.

Film and television may be considered an interweaving between the fantasising and creative Pisces and the electric and universalist Aquarius.

Paradoxical to the holy wars against nations and individuals, charitable acts also blossomed for the first time among groups and entities, including those promoted by the Roman church. Thus, compassion amid religious groups is also a point to note in the Age of Pisces. Schools, convents, religious seclusion and hospitals are, likewise, notable products of this age.

As the transition from one age to another develops, it is proposed that in the Gospel of Luke 22:10, Jesus referred to the Age of Aquarius when replying to the apostles where they should prepare to celebrate the Passover, the holiday that commemorates the freedom of the Israelites from the Egyptians. He replied, *"As you enter the city, a man carrying a jar of water will meet you. Follow him to the house that he enters."*

Age of Aquarius – 2150 to 4300 CE

The Age of Aquarius is not mentioned in the Bible, but a study on the correlation of prophetic periods and the astrological era seems to allude to the culminating spiritual transition the world is to encounter in the first centuries of the third millennium CE.

The Bible, or more specifically, in the Second Epistle of Peter, 8:3 states: *"Dear friends, don't overlook this one fact: With the Lord, one day is like a thousand years and a thousand years like one day."* Knowing that the week has seven days and that the seventh day is the 'Shabbat', this verse may hint that God's week consists of seven thousand years, while His Shabbat lasts for one thousand years.

Taking into consideration that within the biblical framework and chronology the dominant date for the creation of the world was approximately 4000 BCE, the modern-day Hebrew calendar has since the fourth century CE dated the creation to 3761 BCE.[48] This means that Jesus was born 3761 years after the creation of the world. For a random comparison, the Gregorian calendar of 2030 CE converts to the year 5791 in the Hebrew calendar, which reflects the years since creation was presented in the book of Genesis.

According to classical Jewish sources, the Hebrew year 6000 (from sunset of 29 September 2239 until nightfall of 16 September 2240 on the Gregorian calendar) marks the latest time for the initiation of the Messianic Age, which is the future period of time on Earth in which the Messiah will allegedly reign and bring universal peace and brotherhood, without any evil. The Talmud,[49] the Midrash,[50] and the Kabbalistic work Zohar,[51] state that the 'due date' by which the Messiah must appear is 6000 years from creation.

In the book of Exodus, 20:8-10, the fourth commandment states that "six days you shall labour and do all your work" and the seventh day (the Sabbath) "must be kept holy".

Maintaining the statement that each day of the week corresponds to one thousand years of creation: just as the six days of the workweek culminate in the sanctified seventh day of Shabbat, so too will the six millennia of creation culminate in the sanctified seventh millennium, that is, the Messianic Age

(Hebrew years 6000–7000). That line of thought has the sixth millennium of the Hebrew calendar starting approximately in Gregorian calendar's 2240 CE.

The Gospel of Matthew, 20:16 *"The last shall be first and the first last"* may also suggest that the individuals living on Earth at the last part of creation (before the 7th millennia), will be the first ones to experience the new era.

As previously mentioned, astrological ages unfold in waves, comparable to how the four seasons gradually alternate. This explicitly means that a New Age may appear many years before its actual calculated starting date. The ending of an age is likewise not marked by a decade or a century, but by the progressive loss of its pivotal characteristics, as the New Age gradually takes command.

1 degree out of the average 30 degrees that comprise a constellation is accepted in denoting when a certain age begins and another ceases. 1 degree equals 72 years. Therefore, 72 years may be allowed before and after the official year that a transition between ages occurs.

Taking the example of the official (estimated) start of the Age of Aquarius, 2150, it is understood that its first and strong influences on world affairs and society commence in the 2070s, thereupon turning predominantly Aquarian in 2150; and completely terminating the Piscean traits by the 2220s. Nonetheless, the average guideline for a transition, also called the "cusp" period, lies between 2 and 4 degrees, which suggests that Aquarian features have been marginally witnessed since the 2000s.

The first documented acknowledgement that the Age of Aquarius was imminent was the discovery of Aquarius' modern ruling planet, Uranus, in 1781.[52]

In classical Greek mythology, Uranus is the personification of the sky and ruler of the universe. As such, Aquarius universalises all affairs, as it rules the sky and hence all other constellations.

According to astrological theology, Uranus governs ingenuity, scientific inventions, eccentricity, democratic revolutions and liberation. Uranus, the planet of sudden and unexpected changes, also rules electricity, the internet and technology. In society, it rules radical ideas and rebellion, as well as revolutionary events that overturn antiquated norms. In regard to emotions, Uranus induces a sense of universal connection, as observed in groups identified with humanitarian ideals. Nevertheless, the icy giant is the coldest planet in the solar system. Therefore its analytical attitude may reign over mere belief. The constellation of Aquarius, for instance, governs astrology, which despite being a mystical art is also related to meticulous mathematics and systematic geometry.

German astronomer Johann Elert Bode named Uranus after the ancient Greek god of the sky, arguing that as Saturn (Cronus) was the father of Jupiter (Zeus), the new planet should be named after the father of Saturn (Uranus).[53]

Uranus is noticeably unusual amongst the other planets, as it rotates on its side, having its axis of rotation tilted 98 degrees from the plane of the solar system. This causes both hemispheres to alternate between being bathed in light and being in total darkness. Additionally, Uranus rotates clockwise, differing from all other planets in the solar system except for Venus. In astrology, these traits described Uranus as a dissident, non-partisan and an insurgent planet.

In art and literature, Uranus' discovery coincided with romanticism, which emphasised individuality and freedom of creative expression.

Astrological interpretations also associate Uranus with the principles of new or unconventional concepts, individuality, discoveries and democracy.

Aquarius is traditionally ruled by Saturn, a planet commonly characterised by structure and responsibility. Contemporaneously, Aquarius is ruled by Uranus, a planet associated with sudden change and freedom. Combined, the two planets paint the Age of Aquarius in the hues of "the responsibility to change" and "sudden change of structure". Thus, what is understood as the traditional norm may collapse, and humanity is requested to change in order to obtain freedom.

Coinciding with the discovery of Uranus (1781), the Industrial Revolution (1760) bolstered a transformation that the world had never witnessed before. This was a technological period of development that radically remodelled rural and agrarian societies in the Old and New Worlds into industrialised and urbanised regions.

Rebellious movements also occurred, such as the independence of the United States (1776). The event was a self-declared Aquarian aspect of freedom and universalism, as it influenced the rest of the colonies in the Americas to pursue their own independence.

Following the encouragement for liberty, the French Revolution (1787–1799) occurred. A period of great social upheaval in France, aiming to fundamentally alter the relationship between rulers and those they ruled over, as well as to reshape the essence of political authority. The influence of the French Revolution helped to remodel and renew the European and the New World's political establishments.

Other triggers and hints of the Age of Aquarius include the discovery and studies of electricity and its properties, telephone, aviation, modern democracy, space exploration, satellites, computers and genetics.

In the past centuries, entrenched components of the Age of Pisces endeavoured to drift into a more Aquarian fashion. Visual artistry designed by artificial intelligence is in its beginning and, inescapably, cultures will redefine their traditions as computers globalise creation. As a result, music and fashion identity will presumably become universal trends as opposed to local tendencies.

Above all, the Age of Aquarius aims to be constructed on the universalism of knowledge, technology, freedom and the rejection of that which is considered old-fashioned or archaic. The "belief" of Pisces will then be defeated by the "knowledge" of Aquarius.

Aquarius is represented by air, which represents rationality and intellect, and as a result, this age is expected to disseminate information widely. Hence, control is likely to endure in the hands of each individual as opposed to those of absolute leaders, religious organisations or monopolist companies.

If in the eras of Taurus, Aries and Pisces, respectively, the calf, the lamb and the fish were the symbols in the form of an animal, in the Age of Aquarius the symbol becomes the human.

However, this is not meant to extol the human species, but to bring egalitarian status among people. The equality and equity of Aquarius unequivocally extends to all genders, races and species on the planet.

Aquarius is identified with the Greek myth of the beautiful Ganymede, a young man who was the most beautiful human on Earth. Mesmerised by his beauty, Zeus captured the youth so he could be the cupbearer of the gods on Olympus. Such inferential symbolism may associate the ascension of beautiful (benevolent) humans to the highest realms.

In most Indian religions, *samsara* is the 'beginningless' cycle of repeated birth, mundane existence and dying again. Samsara is thought to be suffering, and whatever is unsatisfactory and painful is perpetuated by desire and ignorance, resulting in karma.

Nirvana is the ultimate spiritual goal, and it marks the soteriological release from rebirths in samsara.[54] In the Buddhist tradition, nirvana has commonly been interpreted as the extinction of the "three poisons": greed, aversion and ignorance.[55] Following these lines, it may be tacitly propitious to pair the "three poisons" with zodiac signs commonly associated with such characters: Taurus, Aries and Pisces respectively, where nirvana is achieved in Aquarius. *Nevertheless, this concept is a theory established on coincidence, as opposed to a pragmatic ancient teaching.*

Aquarius rules the etheric fluids, which are often depicted as the water pouring from a jar. More important than pouring the water is Aquarius' condition as the water bearer, which means that Aquarius holds and distributes the ether of life.

Aquarius wields cosmic fluids with such deftness, albeit kindly and equally pouring them to others.

The Age of Pisces is engraved by hues of Virgo throughout its history, as noticed by labour and salaries, laws and rights and hospitals and clinics. Likewise, the Age of Aquarius is surmised to have hues of Leo.

In an example of the combination of Aquarius and Leo, humanity witnessed some negative aspects of the two signs. The pair, in their destructive aspects, led the Nazis to combine Aquarius' Machiavellian technology with Leo's arrogance for power.

Another destructive example of Aquarius motivated by Leo was the invention of the atomic bomb. Einstein's Aquarian $E=mc^2$ equation met Robert Oppenheimer's Leonine direction of a laboratory,[56] where the latter designed the first atomic bombs. In August 1945, these weapons were used in the bombings of Hiroshima and Nagasaki. However, it must also be emphasised that, despite being an Aquarius-Leo aspect, these two occurrences happened during a period where humanity was still morally underdeveloped.

In a spiritually restored world, the submissive line of Pisces, where men are superior to women, one race is superior to another and humans are superior to animals will cease to exist. Aquarius will rebel against self-centredness and selfishness. Not because Aquarius is a better constellation compared to Pisces, but because Aquarius desires the new, eliminating everything that sounds like what was the *status quo* of the previous era. Moreover, mysterious dogmas will have few adherents, losing all their manipulative power.

In the spiritualist parameter, it is advantageous to remember that the Age of Aquarius is to be defined by the emptying of the dense astral regions, since the majority of spirits whose evolutionary levels are not compatible with those of the new Earth, will no longer be able to be reincarnated on this planet. Hence, these spirits of "degrading" personalities are to continue their evolutionary journey on another orb, aligned with their current realities.

Dense astral regions, also known as "lower zones", are one of the dimensions of reality created by the reflection of distorted minds of disembodied spirits.

These regions are commonly darkened, grotesque and insalubrious. There are different lower zones, some of which may be abysmally cruel, where sinister sorcerers and Draconian spirits rule by fear and terror. Others may be seen as similar to the Judaeo-Christian purgatory. Such a perception depends on what the minds of the dwelling spirits may create.

Usually, when incarnated spirits have a malignant and vicious behaviour, which culminates in the agglomeration of antimatter on their souls, they are attracted to these astral regions upon physical death. Following the purging of destructive emotions, those spirits feel "lighter", therefore, they are able to leave such obscure dimensions and progress to higher dimensions for treatment, charitable work and reincarnation. Nonetheless, many remain so, engulfed in remorse or in ideas of vengeance against those who they believe caused their 'misfortunes' during their physical lives.

Aquarius universalises metaphysical knowledge with science and vice versa. Therefore, the emotional and spiritual causes of diseases are to be holistically accepted as official medical reports, conferring advanced genetics – an Aquarian branch of biology – with astral factors.

Leo and its warmth brought the ice age to an end, while Cancer nourished the regions and led humans to fertile places. Gemini disseminated communication and trade, while Taurus crystallised the first civilisations. Aries reorganised the world through authority and war, affirming the planet as a locale of atonement, while Pisces delivered spirituality and belief, despite the suffering and manipulation of the masses.

As it may be noticed, every age that emerged during the recent history of mankind has come to give the previous age continuation, each experiencing the same cycle reflected in a different constellation.

However, the next Age of Aquarius is supposed to be different from the last whole cycle of 25,920 years. Humanity is departing from the group of primitive, preparatory and atoning eras to enter a group of mental, technological and regenerating ones.

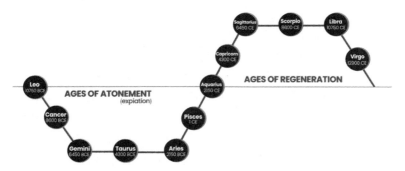

Timeline of the past, present and future astrological ages.

The age of Aquarius should not be understood as a better period as if Aquarius was an exceptionally positive sign compared to all others. What classifies the Age of Aquarius to be the most favourable age so far is the current spiritual evolution of the spirits who populate the Earth. Therefore, Pisces is not to blame, just as Aquarius is not to be congratulated, as the qualities of each era only reflect the population's current level of inner peace and altruism.

Since humanity is experiencing a shift of paradigm, which, presumably is for the common good, Aquarius may provide more of its best aspects as opposed to its worst. In other words, what decides how virtuous or miserable an astrological age shall be is the condition of the spirits who populate the planet. If humans evolve to altruistic habits, the age in which they find themselves will provide the best qualities of that constellation. Accordingly, if the vast population is corrupt and destructive, the astrological age shall, likewise, present its worst features. Thus, it is proposed that the Age of Aquarius is to be highly progressive as humanity is on the brink of consciousness expansion, besides the event that planet Earth is under a new wave of migration of spirits from other enlightened orbs.

Food based on flesh, or food obtained through exploitation, will be seen as barbarism and social prejudice. Moreover, animal-based food will cease to exist even before the height of the Age of Aquarius, and technologies, as well as the discovery of highly nutritious foods, like algae, will be the greatest substitutes for that kind of archaic idea of food.

The paradigm shift will bring an end to mass imprisonment, which will include the end of animal slaughterhouses.

The systematisation of world conventions will also ban the production and sale of meat, as well as other foods obtained through animal exploitation. However, the movement of change will be initiated by the masses themselves, who will wake up from Piscean torpidity in the face of the attentive Aquarian influence.

Racism, sexism and social prejudices will also be seen as moral and spiritual immaturity, pertaining to an embarrassing past.

All in all, Aquarius advances to shift the paradigm and the *status quo*, in a revolution that is to amend the imbalances and animosity among humans and between humanity and animals.

Veganism as Norm

The shift in the "collective conscious" refers to a new era about to begin. However, change does not occur overnight, but gradually. Change starts when the frequency of the collective conscious rises in vibration, thereby resonating with new restoring frequencies from higher dimensions.

As the Earth finds itself in a different reality of consciousness, the individuals and collectives who refrain from adapting to the new way of thinking will be wistfully distressed by the astounding new tendencies that are beginning to replace the old ones.

Natural disasters, such as fires that devastate entire regions, viruses that affect populations worldwide and wars that cause modern-era exodus, serve amongst other reasons, to catapult humanity to a shift of mental frequencies, thereby substantially changing paradigms. These events do not occur as punishment on stagnant consciousnesses who abstain from progressing, but as a means of eliciting the collective conscious to adapt to different behaviours through affliction, since spiritual evolution via charity and compassion continually fails amid most of those who are incarnated in this planet.

This "push" serves as a guarantee that the new frequencies that the planet Earth finds itself in are compatible with its inhabiting societies. It is worth emphasising that natural catastrophes, global epidemics and wars are the materialisations of all that is already occurring to those individuals on an ethereal dimension. In other words, physical materialisations of calamities are condensed circumstances of that which is already a reality somewhere non-physical, and they are neither created by God nor are they the result of divine punishment, but they are collective karma generated by the collective conscious itself.

In the early decades of the 21st century, a multitudinous number of consciousnesses from neighbouring celestial spheres are to migrate to planet Earth, in furtherance of incarnating amid locals. Such movement of new spirits to planet Earth endeavours the propelling of altruistic behaviour, benevolent ideals and the modernisation of societies of all nations.

Comparable migrations have occurred in the past, most notoriously the one that started in the previous Age of Gemini. In those times, spirits native to the Auriga constellation migrated to the planet Earth and, after millennia of polishing their spiritual imperfections, they have, in their majority, gone back to their homeland. Nevertheless, their presence on earth proved essential for the development of technology and a further impulse for science, moral values and the successful perpetuation of humankind.

Spirits from Eta Tauri, a star in the north-west of the Taurus constellation, are gradually permeating the Earth's families and cultures, bringing the essence of altruism to Earth. At an equal pace, earthly spirits identified with animosity, abominable cruelty and those prone to heinous criminality are repeatedly denied reincarnation in the terrestrial sphere.

Conjointly, the average human is welcome to continue their evolution on Earth, evolving through the practice of universal compassion, charity and by virtue of learning via study. There is no such Divine arrangement being placed to refuse certain spirits from reincarnating on Earth. Notwithstanding, their own spiritual frequency will naturally fail to adapt to a world where most inhabitants create a sympathetic and restorative collective conscious.

Considering the proposition of a paradigm shift, veganism emerges as one of the protagonists of a new, egalitarian and morally progressive era.

Veganism is the principle and style of living that suggests the abstention from exploitation, abuse and profiteering of animals for food, entertainment, clothing, sports and laboratory tests.

The adoption of veganism, which proves to be a firm tendency as opposed to a trend, aligns with the frequencies of the Age of Aquarius, which implores equality and universalism of rights, leaving behind all customs that sounds archaic and unjust.

Veganism is still considered taboo among spiritualists and proponents of the "new era," as it could be interpreted as 'non-esoteric' or an agenda promoted by vegan militants. Nevertheless, a small number of spiritualists are attempting to promote the concept, albeit detached from the labels.

As veganism is still a taboo to be addressed in general spiritualistic and esoteric circles, the history of slavery of humans may convey examples of how the turpitudes of society, stationed in denial and egoistical reasoning, supported that system throughout millennia. Regarding slavery in Greece, Egypt, sub-Saharan Africa, Europe and the Americas, argumentation to perpetuate such practice included philosophic, religious and political statements such as "It's natural that some people are slaves;"[57] "Slaves are inferior beings;"[58] "Slavery is good for slaves;"[59] "Some individuals are naturally slaves, hence they need to be ruled;"[60] "Slavery would be rather difficult to abolish;"[60] "Slaves are essential to certain industries;"[61] "Slavery is legal;"[62] "Slavery is supported by the Bible;"[62] "Slavery is acceptable in this culture;"[63] "Living in slavery is better than starving to death;"[64]

Not only is the consolidation of veganism noticed, but also the introduction of practices that are less harmful to the environment, such as the reduction in consumption of pernicious materials, solar and wind power and even the production of electricity from the air. Climate crisis is also triggering a greater interest in self sustainable vehicles and the replacement of various equipment by alternatives less degrading to the planet.

The new winds are to deliver the regenerated Earth with wireless electricity, synthetic antibodies, easily modified genes, practically non-invasive surgeries made by refined lasers, widespread artificial intelligence and the recycling of materials into environmentally friendly alternatives, such as biodegradable goods. The latter will decrease the extraction of natural resources to nearly zero. The replanting of deforested areas and the cleansing of the oceans and soil will also generate many jobs and renew the Earth.

Although the winds of change are likely to be experienced before the calculated years of the new age, they will not be fully experienced before veganism becomes the norm. A plant-based diet is the single biggest step one can take to reduce their environmental impact,[65] which invariably generates collective karma.

It is critical to emphasise that the impact of animal agriculture on the planet is the most serious ecological and moral form of terrorism and subjugation of animals, the land, and, ultimately, humans.

As long as the exploitative industries are financed by humans, the planet Earth can not delve into a completely restored reality – and that includes the locales in the astral dimensions closer to the Earth.

In a scenario where one individual abstains from consuming animal cruelty and is therefore not affected by harmful energy, the same concept can be applied to the whole world.

Veganism has never had such a presence on the face of the Earth before. Neither in Egypt nor in Sumer, neither in China nor in India. Therefore, it is a thrilling moment to experience the rise of a movement endeavouring to finally substitute and rebel against the primitive status quo that holds the planet from evolving to a new era of universal compassion, equality and moral progress.

The vegan movement appears to be humanity's best chance to break the cycle of violence against animals in all of the subjects discussed in this book, such as the atrocities caused by their flesh, the hypocritical use of their symbolism, and sacrifices within many religious cults.

Veganism relates to the principles of equality and respect for every species, proposing their right to exist in freedom. Regardless of labels and nomenclatures, the principles of veganism are one of the most spiritual, sincere and honourable qualities one should hold.

Ultimately, 'spirituality' means being concerned with the spirit and its affairs, as opposed to the material world or physical surroundings. Thus, veganism offers the least paradoxical conduct for those claiming to be on the right side, in furtherance of advancing the planet Earth towards a paradigm shift at a spiritual level.

REFERENCES

Introduction

1 – Lipner, J., (2012). *Hindus: Their Religious Beliefs and Practices.* Sec. ed. Routledge, pp. 263–265.

2 – De Vries, A., (1976). *Dictionary of Symbols and Imagery.* Amsterdam: North–Holland Publishing Company, pp. 85–86.

3 – Brown, R., (1991). Ganesh: *Studies of an Asian God.* Albany: State University of New York.

4 – Milner, E., (2010). *A Dialogue on Christianity.* iUniverse.

5 – Wilby, E., (2005). *Cunning Folk and Familiar Spirits: Shamanistic Visionary Traditions in Early Modern British Witchcraft and Magic.* Brighton: Sussex Academic Press.

6 – Watanabe, H., Fujiyama, A. et al. (2004). The International Chimpanzee Chromosome 22 Consortium., DNA sequence and comparative analysis of chimpanzee chromosome 22. *Nature* 429, pp. 382–388. [Accessed 12th of July 2019].

The Souls of Animals

1 – Koch, C., (2004). *The Quest for Consciousness: A Neurobiological Approach.* Roberts & Co., pp. 105–116.

2 –   Beyssade, J-M., (1992). *The Idea of God and Proofs of His Existence in The Cambridge Companion to Descartes.* Cambridge: Cambridge University Press, pp. 174–199.

3 –   Dittrich, W. and Gies H., (2000). Probing the Quantum Vacuum: *Perturbative Effective Action Approach in Quantum Electrodynamics and its Application.* Berlin: Springer.

4 –   Barreto, D., (2019). God. *The Supernatural Science: Theory and Magic.* London.

5 –   Silver, C. B., (1998). *Strange and Secret Peoples: Fairies and Victorian Consciousness.* Oxford University Press USA.

6 –   Sheldrake, R., (2011). *The Presence of the Past: Morphic Resonance and the Habits of Nature.* London: Icon Books.

7 –   Lipton, B. H., Bensch K. G. and Karasek M. A., (1991). Differentiation. *Microvessel Endothelial Cell Trans-differentiation: Phenotypic Characterization.* 46:117–133.

Karma and Reincarnation

1 –   Barreto, D., (2019). Karma. *The Supernatural Science: Theory and Magic.* London, pp. 61-67.

2 –   Heibron, J. L., (1985). *Bohr's First Theories of the Atom;* Kennedy, A. P.; P. J., 1985. *Niels Bohr: A Centenary Volume.* Cambridge, Massachusetts: Harvard University Press, pp. 33–49.

3 –   Xavier F. C. and Emmanuel, (1939). The Adamic Races. *On the Way to The Light.* Brasilia: International Spiritist Council, pp. 27-34.

Animals and Metaphysics

1 – Holler, F. J., Skoog D. A. and Crouch, S. R., (2007). *Principles of Instrumental Analysis.* 6th ed. Cengage Learning, p. 9.

2 – Barreto, D., (2019). Oracles. *The Supernatural Science: Theory and Magic.* London, pp. 143-149.

3 – Kanev, I., *et al.* (2013). Electrical Components of Chromosomes. *Searching for Electrical Properties, Phenomena and Mechanisms in the Construction and Function of Chromosomes.* Volume 6, Issue 7. Amsterdam: Computational and Structural Biotechnology Journal.

4 – Hess M., *et al.* (2012). *Are the Structural and Functional Similarity Between the Human Chromosomes and the Electrical Transformer Coincidental.* Omaha: University of Nebraska Medical Center, Munroe-Meyer Institute, Human Genetics Laboratory Omaha.

5 – Zhao Y. and Zhan, Q., (2012). *Electric Fields Generated by Synchronized Oscillations of Microtubules, Centrosomes and Chromosomes Regulate the Dynamics of Mitosis and Meiosis.* 2–9(1): 26. Theoretical Biology and Medical Modelling.

6 – Zhao Y., Zhan Q., (2012). *Electric Oscillation and Coupling of Chromatin Regulate Chromosome Packaging and Transcription in Eukaryotic Cells.* 3–9(1): 27. Theoretical Biology and Medical Modelling.

7 – O'Hara A.M., Shanahan F., (2006). *The Gut Flora as a Forgotten Organ.* 7 (7): 688–93. EMBO Reports.

8 – Lodish, H., *et al.* (2000). Chemical Equilibrium. *Molecular Cell Biology.* 4th edition. New York: W. H. Freeman.

9 –   Sheldrake, R., (2011). *The Presence of the Past: Morphic Resonance and the Habits of Nature.* London: Icon Books.

10 –   Wiltschko, F. R. and Wiltschko, W., (2012). Magnetoreception. In Larrea, C., ed.: *Sensing in Nature. Advances in Experimental Medicine and Biology, n.* 739. Springer.

11 –   Walcott, C., (1996). *Pigeon Homing: Observations, Experiments and Confusions.* 199 (Pt 1): 21–7. The Journal of Experimental Biology.

12 –   Gould, J. L., (1984). *Magnetic Field Sensitivity in Animals.* 46: 585–98. Annual Review of Physiology.

13 –   Lilly, J., (1987). *Communication Between Man and Dolphin: The Possibilities of Talking with Other Species.* Julian Press.

14 –   Persians, et al. (5th–4th century BCE). King James. Chapter 2. *First Testament.* Jonah.

15 –   Bruckner, J., (2004). *NIV Application Commentary: Jonah, Nahum, Habakkuk, Zephaniah.* Grand Rapids: Zondervan.

16 –   Lima S.L. and O'Keefe, J.M., (2013). *Do Predators Influence the Behaviour of Bats?* 88 (3): 626–44. Biological Reviews of the Cambridge Philosophical Society.

Spiritual Repercussions of Eating Meat

1 –   Dirac, P., (1965). *Physics Nobel Lectures.* 12. Amsterdam–London–New York: Elsevier. 12, pp. 320–325.

2 –   Eisberg, R. and Resnick, R., (1985). *Quantum Physics of Atoms, Molecules, Solids, Nuclei, and Particles.* (2nd ed.).John Wiley & Sons. pp. 59–60.

3 –   Norwood, F. B. and Lusk, J. L., (2010). *Direct Versus Indirect Questioning: An Application to the Well–Being of Farm*

Animals. 96 (3): 551–565. Social Indicators Research, pp. 551-565.

4 – Noore K. L.; Agur, A.M., (2007). *Essential Clinical Anatomy.* (3rd ed.).Lippincott, p. 181.

5 – Sender, R., Fuchs, S. and Milo, R., (2016). *Revised Estimates for the Number of Human and Bacteria Cells in the Body.* 14(8). PLOS Biology.

6 – Lipton, B., (2015). *The Biology of Belief.* UK ed. London: Hay House.

7 – Dittrich W. and Gies, H., (2000). *Probing the Quantum Vacuum: Perturbative Effective Action Approach.* Berlin: Springer.

8 – Barreto, D., (2019). God. *The Supernatural Science: Theory and Magic.* London, pp. 12–19.

9 – Gribbin, J., (2000). *Q is for Quantum –   An Encyclopedia of Particle Physics.* New York: Simon & Schuster.

10 – Gauss, C. F., (1801). *The Shaping of Arithmetic After Disquisitiones Arithmeticae.* (Latin vers.), p. 235.

11 – Sheldrake, R., (2011). *The Presence of the Past: Morphic Resonance and the Habits of Nature.* London: Icon Books.

Behind Animal Sacrifice

1 – Flores, D., (1999). *The Funerary Sacrifice of Animals During the Pre-dynastic Period.* Ottawa. The University of Toronto.

2 – Burkert, W., (1983). *Homo Necans: The Anthropology of Ancient Greek Sacrificial Ritual and Myth.* Translated by P. Bing. Berkeley: Univ. of California Press.

3 – Rüpke, J., (2007). *A Companion to Roman Religion.* Blackwell Publishing. Pp. 263–71.

4 –   Fuller, C., (2004). The Camphor Flame: Popular Hinduism and Society in India. Princeton University Press. pp. 46, 83–85.

5 –   Place, R. and Guiley, R., (2009) *Magic and Alchemy*. Chelsea House Publishers.

6 –   Barreto, D., (2019). Offering and Sacrifice. *The Supernatural Science: Theory and Magic*. London.

Animal Worship in Ancient Religions

1 –   Wilkinson, H., (1999). *Early Dynastic Egypt*. London: Routledge.

2 –   Redford, D., (2001). Nut. *The Oxford Encyclopedia of Ancient Egypt*. USA: Oxford University Press.

3 –   Ikram, S., *et al.* (2015). Fatal Force–Feeding or Gluttonous Gagging? The Death of Kestrel. (Stellenbosch University). Volume 63. *Journal of Archaeological Science*, pp. 72–77.

4 –   McKnight, L. M., *et al.* (2015). Application of Clinical Imaging and 3D Printing to the Identification of Anomalies in an Ancient Egyptian Animal Mummy. Volume 3. *Journal of Archaeological Science,* pp. 328–332.

5 –   Baldwin, J. A., (1975). *Notes and Speculations on the Domestication of the Cat in Egypt*. Anthropos. Nomos Verlagsgesellschaft, pp. 428-448.

6 –   Ikram, S., (2015). *Speculations on the Role of Animal Cults in the Economy of Ancient Egypt*. In Massiera, M., Mathieu, B. and Rouffet, F., (2015).*Apprivoiser Le Sauvage / Taming the Wild. Montpellier: Cahiers de l'Égypte Nilotique et Méditerranéenne,* pp. 211–228.

7 –   Engels, D. W., (1999). Egypt. *Classical Cats. The Rise and Fall of the Sacred Cat.* London, New York: Routledge, pp. 18–47.

8 –   Burton, A., (1973). Chapter 4. *Diodorus Siculus.* Book 1: A Commentary. Leiden: Brill, pp. 38–42.

9 –   Tomorad, M., (2015). The Prohibition of Paganism in Egypt From the Middle of the 4th to the Middle of the 6th Century CE. *The End of Ancient Egyptian Religion.* Vol. IV. The Journal of Egyptological Studies, pp. 147–167.

10 –   Michaels, A., (2004). *Hinduism: Past and Present.* Princeton, New Jersey: Princeton University Press.

11 –   Shastri, J. L., (1950). Siva Purana. (Eng. transl.).Part 1. Motilal Banarsidass.

12 –   *Gods in Shackles. (2016). Directed by* Iyer, S. and Cook, D. India–Canada. [Viewed 4th of September 2019].

13 –   Nidhin T., (3rd of July 2016). *"Gods in Shackles Strikes a Tender Chord".* Deccan Chronicle. <https://www.deccan-chronicle.com/> [Accessed 4th of September 2019].

14 –   Lochtefeld, G., (2001). *The Illustrated Encyclopedia of Hinduism.* Rosen Publishing, pp. 224; 265; 520.

15 –   Fuller, C. J., (2004). *The Camphor Flame: Popular Hinduism and Society in India.* (Rev. ed.).Princeton University Press, p. 83.

16 –   Balmurli, N. & Suraj, J., (2018). 'Provincialising' Vegetarianism Putting Indian Food Habits in Their Place. *Economic and political weekly.* 53.

17 –   Laveesh, B., (2009). Indian States at a Glance, 2008. Performance, Facts and Figures – West Bengal: Pearson Education India, p. 30.

18 –   Fuller, M. F., (2004). *The Encyclopedia of Farm Animal Nutrition*. Wallingford: Centre for Agriculture and Bioscience International, p. 589.

19 –   Sample Registration, (2014). Religion. *National System Baseline Survey 2014*. India: Census India. <http://censusindia.gov.in> [Accessed: 5th of September 2019].

20 –   Department of Animal Husbandry & Dairying, (2019). *Dairying and Fisheries*. India: Ministry of Agriculture & Farmers' Welfare. Government of India. Annual Report 2018–19. <http://dahd.nic.in/documents/reports> [Accessed: 30th of July 2020].

21 –   Keightley, D., (1999). *The Shang: China's First Historical Dynasty*. In Loewe M. and Shaughnessy E., 22

22 –   Yuan, J. and Flad, R., (2005). *New Zoo-archaeological Evidence for Changes in Shang Dynasty Animal Sacrifice*. Vol. 24, Is. 3. Institute of Archaeology, Chinese Academy of Social Sciences; Department of Anthropology, Harvard University, pp 252–270.

23 -   (1999).*The Cambridge History of Ancient China:* From the Origins of Civilization to 221 BCE. Cambridge: Cambridge University Press, pp. 232-291.

24 –   Loewe M. and Shaughnessy E., (1999). *The Cambridge History of Ancient China:* From the Origins of Civilization to 221 BCE. Cambridge: Cambridge University Press.

25 –   Ahlfort, K., (2011). *Genetic Study Confirms: First Dogs Came from East Asia*. Royal Institute of Technology news release. Uppsala University.

26 –   Wayne, R. and Vonholdt, B., (2012). *Evolutionary Genomics of Dog Domestication*. Mammalian Genome. Department

of Ecology & Evolutionary Biology. Los Angeles: University of California.

27 – Fingarette, H., (1972). Confucius: *The Secular as Sacred.* New York: Harper.

28 – Chen, Y., (2012). Confucionismo como religião: controvérsias e consequências. Brill.

29 – Adler, J., (1999). Response to Taylor, R., 1986. *Of Animals And Man: The Confucian Perspective.* Conference on Religion and Animals. Cambridge: Harvard–Yenching Institute.

30 – Creel, H. G., (1982). *What Is Taoism? And Other Studies in Chinese Cultural History.* Chicago: University of Chicago Press.

31 – Anderson, E. N.; Raphals, L., (2007). Daoism and Animals. *A Communion of Subjects: Animals in Religion, Science, and Ethics.* Evergreen University, Washington, pp. 275–290.

32 – Harvey, P., (2000). *An Introduction to Buddhist Ethics: Foundations, Values and Issues.* Cambridge University Press.

33 – Phelps, N., (2004). *The Great Compassion: Buddhism & Animal Rights.* New York: Lantern Books, p. 76.

34 – Nelson, J. K., (1996). *A Year in the Life of a Shinto Shrine.* Seattle–London: University of Washington Press.

35 – Offner, C. B., (1979). *Shinto.* In Anderson N. (1960).*The World's Religions* (fourth ed.). Leicester: Inter–Varsity Press, pp. 191–218.

36 – Bocking, B., (1997). *A Popular Dictionary of Shinto.*(revised ed.).Richmond: Curzon.

37 –   Ishige, Naomichi (2001). *The History and Culture of Japanese Food.* New York: Columbia University Press.

Animals in Mysticism

1 –   Aldred, L., (2000). *Plastic Shamans and Astroturf Sun Dances: New Age Commercialization of Native American Spirituality* in: *The American Indian Quarterly* 24.3. Lincoln: University of Nebraska Press, pp. 329–352.

2 –   Goldenweiser A., (1910). *Totemism: An analytical study.* 23, Journal of American Folk-Lore, pp. 179–293.

3 –   Barreto, D., (2019). Offerings. *The Supernatural Science: Theory and Magic.* London.

4 –   Sheldrake, R., (2011). *The Presence of the Past: Morphic Resonance and the Habits of Nature.* London: Icon Books.

5 –   Ashcroft, F., (2002). *Life at the Extremes: The Science of Survival.* University of California Press, p. 112.

6 –   Blavatsky, H. P., (1889). *The Key to Theosophy.* London: The Theosophical Publishing Company.

7 –   Brown, F., *et al.* (1849). *The Brown-Driver-Briggs Hebrew and English Lexicon. (rep. 1991).*Hendrickson, p. 521.

8 –   Bird, R., *et al.* (2007). *Transport Phenomena.* (2nd ed.).John Wiley & Sons, p. 266.

9 –   Linsley, J., *et al.* (1997). Space Air Watch: *Observation of the Earth Atmosphere from the ISSA Space Station.* Vol. 5. International Cosmic Ray Conference. NASA Astrophysics Data System, p. 385.

10 –   Teeter, E., et al. (2000). *A History of the Animal World in the Ancient Near East.* Vol. 64, Boston: Brill.

11 – Berresford, P., (1998). *The Ancient World of the Celts.* (2003 edn.).London: Robinson Publishing, p. 175.

12 – Green, M., (1992). *Animals in Celtic Life and Myth.* London: Routledge.

13 – Green, M., (2005). *Exploring the World of the Druids.* London: Thames & Hudson.

14 – Wilby, E., (2005). *Cunning Folk and Familiar Spirits: Shamanistic Visionary Traditions in Early Modern British Witchcraft and Magic.* Brighton: Sussex Academic Press.

15 – Willis, D., (1995). *Malevolent Nurture.* New York: Cornell University Press, pp. 32, 52.

16 – Audi, R., (1995). *Cambridge Dictionary of Philosophy.* Cambridge; New York: Cambridge University Press, p. 355.

17 – Various, (1973). *The Encyclopedia of Philosophy.* New York: Macmillan.

18 – Jung, C., (1960). *Instinct and the Unconscious. Vol. 8,* Collected Works, pp. 137–138.

19 – Singer, J., (1968). *Culture and the Collective Unconscious.* Evanston: Northwestern University Press, pp. 36–37.

20 – Greenwald, A. G., Klinger, M. R. and Schuh, E. S., (1995). Activation by Marginally Perceptible Stimuli. *Dissociation of Unconscious From Conscious Cognition.* General, 124(1). Journal of experimental psychology, p.22.

21 – Lodish, H., Berk, A. and Zipursky, S. L., (2000). Molecular Cell Biology: Section 21.4. *Neurotransmitters, Synapses, and Impulse Transmission.* (4th ed.) New York: W. H. Freeman.

22 – Schultz W., (2015). Neuronal Reward and Decision Signals. *From Theories to Data*. Vol. 95, n. 3. In Physiological Reviews, pp. 853–951.

23 – Berridge KC, Robinson TE. Liking, wanting, and the incentive-sensitization theory of addiction. *Am Psychol.* 2016 Nov;71(8):670-679. doi: 10.1037/amp0000059. PMID: 27977239; PMCID: PMC5171207.

24 – A. L. Frothingham, (1916). "Babylonian Origin of Hermes the Snake-God, and of the Caduceus I". *American Journal of Archaeology*. 20, No. 2 (April–June 1916) (2): 175–211

25 – Stahuljak, Z (2013). "Symbolic Archaeology". Pornographic Archaeology: *Medicine, Medievalism, and the Invention of the French Nation*. Philadelphia: De Gruyter/University of Pennsylvania Press]

Planetary Transformation

1 – Food and Agriculture Organization of the United Nations, (2017). *Data of Land Animals Slaughtered.* FAOSTAT. <http://faostat3.fao.org> [Accessed 27th of September 2019].

2 – Food and Agriculture Organization of the United Nations, (2011). *Fishery and Aquaculture Statistics. FAO* <http://www.fao.org/3/i3507t/i3507t.pdf> [Accessed 27th of September 2019].

3 – Pinto, C., et al. (2014). *Casualties Distribution in Human and Natural Hazards.* Mathematical Methods in Engineering. Springer Netherlands. pp. 173–180.

4 – Joos, G., (1951). T*heoretical Physics.* London– Glasgow: Blackie and Son, p. 679.

5 – Slipher, V. M., (1ˢᵗ of January 1913). The radial velocity of the Andromeda Nebula. *Galaxies: Motion in Line of Sight: Andromeda Galaxy.* Lowell Observatory Bulletin. Astrophysics Data System – Harvard University.

6 – Friedmann, A., (1999). General Relativity and Gravitation. *On the Curvature of Space.*

7 – Lemaître, G., (1927). *A Homogeneous Universe of Constant Mass and Increasing Radius Accounting For the Radial Speed of Extra–galactic Nebulae.* Transl. Université catholique de Louvain. Astrophysics Data System – Harvard University.

8 – Philipp, G., et al. (2018). 'Did Our Species Evolve in Subdivided Populations across Africa, and Why Does It Matter?' Trends in Ecology & Evolution. *33 (8). Cell,* pp. 582–594.

9 – Klein, R., (1995). Anatomy, Behaviour, and Modern Human Origins. 9 (2) *Journal of World Prehistory,* pp. 167–198.

10 – McBrearty, S. and Brooks, A., (2000). The Revolution That Wasn't: A New Interpretation of the Origin of Modern Human Behaviour. *Journal of Human Evolution,* 39 (5), pp. 453–563.

11 – Henshilwood, C. and Marean, C., (2003). The Origin of Modern Human Behavior: Critique of the Models and Their Test Implications. *Current Anthropology.* 44 (5), pp. 627–651.

12 – Harvati, K., et al. (2019). 'Apidima Cave fossils provide earliest evidence of Homo sapiens in Eurasia', *Nature,* pp. 571, 500–504.

13 – Zeder, M., (2011). 'The Origins of Agriculture in the Near East'. *Current Anthropology.* 52 (S4), pp. 221–235.

14 – Tudge, C., (1998). Neanderthals, Bandits and Farmers: How Agriculture Really Began. New Haven: Yale University Press.

15 – Noble, T., et al. (2013). *Western Civilization: Beyond Boundaries*. Cengage Learning.

16 – Walker, M., et al. (2009). "Formal definition and dating of the Global Stratotype Section and Point For the Base of the Holocene Using the Greenland NGRIP Ice Core and Selected Auxiliary Records" *Journal of Quaternary Science*, 24 (1), pp. 3–17.

17 – Bellwood, P., (2004). *First Farmers: The Origins of Agricultural Societies*. Wiley–Blackwell, p. 384.

18 – Andersen, B. and Borns, H., (1997). *'The Ice Age World: An Introduction to Quaternary History and Research With Emphasis on North America and Northern Europe During the Last 2.5 Million Years'*. Oslo: Universitetsforlaget.

19 – Deutscher, G., (2007). *Syntactic Change in Akkadian: The Evolution of Sentential Complementation*. Oxford University Press US, pp. 20–21.

20 – Xavier F. C. and Emmanuel, (1939). The Adamic Races. *On the Way to The Light*. Brasilia: International Spiritist Council, pp. 30–33.

21 – Kramer, S., (1988). *In the World of Sumer: An Autobiography*. Detroit: Wayne State University Press, p. 44.

22 – Kramer, S., (1988). *History Begins at Sumer: Thirty–Nine Firsts in Recorded History*. 3rd edition. Philadelphia: University of Pennsylvania Press, pp. 52–55.

23 – Nissen, H., Damerow, P. and Englund, R., (1993). *Archaic Bookkeeping: Early Writing and Techniques of Economic*

Administration in the Ancient Near East. Chicago: University of Chicago Press.

24 – Moses, et al. (6th century BCE). Exodus. The Golden Calf. *Old Testament.* C. 32, vers. 1–5.

25 – López, A., (1998). *Sahagún.* In Sahagún, B., (1577). 'General History of the Things of New Spain. *The Florentine Codex.'* Pp. 10, 48.

26 – Lazaridis, I., et al. (2017). "Genetic Origins of the Minoans and Mycenaeans". *Nature*, pp. 2–3.

27 – Osborne, R., (2009). *Greece in the Making: 1200–479 BCE.* London: Routledge, p. 17.

28 – Barton, J., (1998), *The Cambridge Companion to Biblical Interpretation.* Cambridge: Cambridge University Press.

29 – Coogan, M., (2009). *A Brief Introduction to the Old Testament.* Oxford: Oxford University Press.

30 – Langdon, S. and Gardiner, A., (1920). "The Treaty of Alliance Between Hattusili, King of the Hittites and the Pharaoh Ramesses II of Egypt". *Journal of Egyptian Archaeology.* 6 (3), pp. 179–205.

31 – Waldbaum, J., (1978). *From Bronze to Iron: The Transition From the Bronze Age to the Iron Age in the Eastern Mediterranean. Studies in Mediterranean Archaeology. Philadelphia:* Coronet Books Inc.

32 – *The Story of India With Michael Wood.* BBC Worldwide, 2007. [Viewed 26th of November 2019].

33 – Sharma, C., (1962). Chronological Summary of History of Indian Philosophy. *Indian Philosophy: A Critical Survey.* New York: Barnes & Noble, p. 6.

34 –   Avesta (1500 BCE–1000 BCE). Ahunuvaiti Gatha. *Yasna.* 31. vers. 8.

35 –   Ridley, R. T., (2019). *Akhenaten: A Historian's View. The History of Ancient Egypt.* Cairo–New York: The American University in Cairo Press.

36 –   Moses, et al. (6th century BCE). Exodus. The Golden Calf. *Old Testament.* C. 32, vers. 1–5.

37 –   Stager, L. and Wolff, S. R., (1984). "Child Sacrifice at Carthage – Religious Rite or Population Control?" *Biblical Archaeology Review.* 10:1.

38 –   Shephard, S., (2012). *The Prophetic Seventy Weeks Solved. Vancouver:* Castle Publishing.

39 –   Schürer, E., (1896). Vol. I, Herod the Great. *A History of the Jewish People in the Time of Jesus Christ.* New York: Scribner's, pp. 400–467.

40 –   Murray, A., (1986). "Medieval Christmas". 36 (12). *History Today,* pp. 31–39.

41 –   MacMullen R., (1997). *Christianity and Paganism in the Fourth to Eighth Centuries. New Haven:* Yale University Press.

42 –   Burke–Gaffney, W., (1937). "Kepler and the Star of Bethlehem". 31, *Journal of the Royal Astronomical Society of Canada, p.* 417.

43 –   Ortíz C. and Rodríguez, M. C., (1999). *"Olmec Ritual Behavior at El Manatí: A Sacred Space"* (ed.) Grove, D. and Joyce, R. A., (1999). *Social Patterns in Pre-Classic Mesoamerica.* Washington, D.C: Dumbarton Oaks, pp. 225 –   254.

44 – Scherer, A. K., (2015). *Mortuary Landscapes of the Classic Maya: Rituals of Body and Soul.* Austin: University of Texas Press.

45 – Sanchez, C., (1993). *"Funerary Practices and Human Sacrifice in Teotihuacan Burials"* (ed.) Berrin, K. And Pasztory, E. (1993). *Teotihuacan, Art from the City of the Gods.* London: Thames and Hudson. Fine Arts Museums of San Francisco, p. 113–114.

46 – Bernardino de Sahagún, (2006). 'General History of the Things of New Spain. *The Florentine Codex'*, (2006 ed.) Ángel, M. Editorial Porrúa, p. 97.

47 – Fitzgerald, A. J., (2010). A Social History of the Slaughterhouse: From Inception to Contemporary Implications. Department of Sociology and Anthropology. *Research in Human Ecology.* Vol. 17. Windsor: University of Windsor.

48 – Young's Analytical Concordance of the Holy Bible, 1879, 8th Edition, 1939—entry under 'Creation' quoting Dr. William Hales New Analysis of Chronology and Geography, History and Prophecy, Vol. 1, 1830, p. 210.

49 – Babylonian Talmud Rosh Hashana 31a and Sanhedrin 97a

50 – Pirke De Rabbi Eliezer, Gerald Friedlander, Sepher-Hermon Press, New York, 1981, p. 141.

51 – Zohar (1:117a) and Zohar Vayera 119a

52 – Jegatheesan R., (2013). Uranus: Discovery of the Seventh Planet in Sun family, 26th of April, 1781. 4 (10), *Discovery*, pp. 3-4.

53 – Littmann, M., (2004). *Planets Beyond: Discovering the Outer Solar System.* Courier Dover Publications, pp. 10–11.

54 – Buswell Jr., et al. (2013). *The Princeton Dictionary of Buddhism.* Princeton: Princeton University Press.

55 – Keown, D., (2003). *A Dictionary of Buddhism. Oxford:* Oxford University Press.

56 – Hewlett, R., Anderson, O., (1962). *The New World, 1939–1946. A History of the United States Atomic Energy Commission.* University Park: Pennsylvania State University Press.

57 – White, D., (2012). *Freedom on My Mind: A History of African Americans with Documents.* Beech Cottage: Bedford Books.

58 – Taylor, M., (2016) British Proslavery Arguments and the Bible, 1823–1833, *Slavery & Abolition,* 37:1, pp. 139-158.

59 – De Wet, C. L., (2016). "The Punishment of Slaves in Early Christianity: The Views of Some Selected Church Fathers". *Acta Theologica.* 23 (1): p. 263.

60 – Goodey, C. F. "Politics, Nature, and Necessity: Were Aristotle's Slaves Feeble Minded?" Political Theory 27, no. 2 (1999): 203-24. <http://www.jstor.org/stable/191829> [Accessed 17th of December 2019].

61 – Hampton, G., (2015). *Imagining Slaves and Robots in Literature, Film, and Popular Culture.* Lexington Book, p. 25.

62 – Ingersoll, j., (2015). *Building God's Kingdom: Inside the World of Christian Reconstruction.* Oxford University Press, p. 205.

63 – Rushdoony, R. J., (1973). *The Institutes of Biblical Law,* 1 p. 137.

64 – *Aristotle, Politics,* 1254b 16–21; in: Aristotle (1985). The Politics. (Transl.) Lord, C., University of Chicago Press, p. 41.

65 – *Science*, 01 Jun 2018: Vol. 360, Issue 6392. Reducing food's environmental impacts through producers and consumers. pp. 987-992. DOI: 10.1126/science.aaq0216

Further Reading

Barreto, D., (2019). *The Supernatural Science: Theory and Magic.*

Bessant, A., Leadbeater C. W., (1901). *Thought-Forms.*

Parker, D. & J., (2009). *Parkers' Encyclopedia of Astrology.* Watkins Publishing.

Grant, C., (2006). *The No-nonsense Guide to Animal Rights.*

Story, Francis (1964). *The Place of Animals in Buddhism.* Buddhist Publication Society.

Henrich, J., & McElreath, R., (2007). *Dual Inheritance Theory: The Evolution of Human Cultural Capacities and Cultural Evolution.* In R. Dunbar & L. Barrett (Eds.), Oxford Handbook of Evolutionary Psychology (pp. 555–570). Oxford University Press.

Kemmerer, Lisa (2012). *Animals and World Religions.* Oxford University Press.

White, C., (2016). *The Cognitive Foundations of Reincarnation.* Method & Theory in the Study of Religion, 28(3).

Hodge, K. M., (2008). *Descartes' Mistake: How Afterlife Beliefs Challenge the Assumption that Humans are Intuitive Cartesian Substance Dualists.* Journal of Cognition and Culture, 8(3), pp. 387–415.

Boyer, P., (2003). *Religious thought and behaviour as by-products of brain function.* Trends in Cognitive Sciences, 7(3), 119–124.

Henrich, J., & McElreath, R., (2007). *Dual Inheritance Theory: The Evolution of Human Cultural Capacities and Cultural Evolution.* In R. Dunbar & L. Barrett (Eds.), Oxford Handbook of Evolutionary Psychology (pp. 555–570). Oxford University Press.

Houston, Stephen D., (2004). *The First Writing: Script Invention as History and Process.* Cambridge: Cambridge University Press.

Kozłowski, Stefan Karol (1999). *The Eastern Wing of the Fertile Crescent: Late Prehistory of Greater Mesopotamian Lithic Industries.* Oxford: Archaeopress, 1999.

Penrose, Roger (2016). *Fashion, Faith, and Fantasy in the New Physics of the Universe.* Princeton University Press.

Padmanabh, S., (1998). *The Jaina Path of Purification.*

Barkow, J., Cosmides, L., & Tooby, J. (Eds.). (1992). *The Adapted Mind: Evolutionary Psychology and the generation of culture.* New York, NY: Oxford University Press.

Purzycki, B. G., & Willard, A. K., (2016). *MCI theory: a critical discussion. Religion, Brain & Behavior.* 6(3), pp. 207–248.

Banerjee, K., & Bloom, P., (2013). *Would Tarzan believe in God? Conditions for the emergence of religious belief. Trends in Cognitive Sciences.* 17(1), 7–8.

Guthrie, S., (1995). Faces in the Clouds: A New Theory of Religion. Oxford University Press.

Jong, J., Halberstadt, J. & Bluemke, M., (2012). Foxhole atheism, revisited: The effects of mortality salience on explicit and implicit religious belief. Journal of Experimental Social Psychology, 48(5), 983–989. https://doi.org/10.1016/j.jesp.2012.03.005

Guthrie, S., (1995). Faces in the Clouds: A New Theory of Religion. Oxford University Press.

Wilson, D. S., (2003). Darwin's Cathedral: Evolution, Religion, and the Nature of Society (1 edition). Chicago: University Of Chicago Press.

McCauley, R. N., & Lawson, E. T., (2002). *Bringing Ritual to Mind: Psychological Foundations of Cultural Forms.* Cambridge, UK. Cambridge University Press.

Pathak S., (2013). *Figuring Religions: Comparing Ideas, Images and Activities.* Albany, NY. University of New York Press.

Norris, P., & Inglehart, R., (2012). Sacred and Secular: Religion and Politics Worldwide (2nd edition). Cambridge: Cambridge University Press.

Boyer, P., (1994). *The Naturalness of Religious Ideas:* A Cognitive Theory of Religion. Berkeley: University of California Press.

Slone, D. J., (2004). *Theological Incorrectness: Why Religious People Believe What They Shouldn't* (1st edition). Oxford; New York: Oxford University Press.

Järnefelt, E., Canfield, C. F. & Kelemen, D., (2015). *The divided mind of a disbeliever:* Intuitive beliefs about nature as purposefully created among different groups of non-religious adults. Cognition, 140, 72-88.

Made in the USA
Columbia, SC
29 August 2021

44532454R00134